Acronyms for eBay Buyers

- *ARC:* Advance Readers Copy (paperback version of a book that is released early for publicity purposes)
- *COA:* Certificate of authenticity
- *CONUS:* Continental United States (the *continental* United States includes Alaska, but not Hawaii, while the *contiguous* United States excludes both Alaska and Hawaii)
- *DOA:* Dead on arrival (the item doesn't work out of the package)
- *FB:* Feedback
- *GP:* Gold plate
- *GWP:* Gift with purchase
- *HGE:* Heavy Gold Electroplated
- *INIT:* Initials
- *ISBN:* International Standard Book Number (used to identify books)
- *LCD:* Liquid Crystal Display
- *LE:* Limited Edition
- *LTD:* Made in a limited quantity
- *MIB:* Mint in box
- *MIJ:* Made in Japan
- *MIMB:* Mint in mint box
- *MIP:* Mint in package
- *MNB:* Mint, no box
- *MOC:* Mint on card
- *MOMC:* Mint on mint card

- *MONMC:* Mint on near mint card
- *MOP:* Mother of pearl
- *MWBT:* Mint with both tags
- *MWMT:* Mint with mint tags
- *NARU:* Not a registered user (suspended eBay user)
- *NM:* Near mint
- *NORES:* No reserve price on auction
- *NOS:* New, old stock
- *NR:* No reserve price on auction — highest bid wins
- *NRFB:* Never removed from box
- *NWOT:* New without tags
- *NWT:* New with tags
- *OEM:* Original equipment manufacturer
- *OOAK:* One of a kind
- *OOP:* Out of print, out of production
- *PM:* Priority Mail
- *RS:* Rhinestones
- *S/O:* Sold out
- *TM:* Trademark
- *UPC:* Universal Product Code (a unique machine-readable identifier for products)
- *USPS:* United States Postal Service
- *VHTF:* Very hard to find

eBay® Bargain Shopping For Dummies®

Cheat Sheet

eBay Time in the Continental U.S.

eBay	Pacific	Mountain	Central	Eastern
0:00	12:00 a.m.	1:00 a.m.	2:00 a.m.	3:00 a.m.
1:00	1:00 a.m.	2:00 a.m.	3:00 a.m.	4:00 a.m.
2:00	2:00 a.m.	3:00 a.m.	4:00 a.m.	5:00 a.m.
3:00	3:00 a.m.	4:00 a.m.	5:00 a.m.	6:00 a.m.
4:00	4:00 a.m.	5:00 a.m.	6:00 a.m.	7:00 a.m.
5:00	5:00 a.m.	6:00 a.m.	7:00 a.m.	8:00 a.m.
6:00	6:00 a.m.	7:00 a.m.	8:00 a.m.	9:00 a.m.
7:00	7:00 a.m.	8:00 a.m.	9:00 a.m.	10:00 a.m.
8:00	8:00 a.m.	9:00 a.m.	10:00 a.m.	11:00 a.m.
9:00	9:00 a.m.	10:00 a.m.	11:00 a.m.	12:00 p.m.
10:00	10:00 a.m.	11:00 a.m.	12:00 p.m.	1:00 p.m.
11:00	11:00 a.m.	12:00 p.m.	1:00 p.m.	2:00 p.m.
12:00	12:00 p.m.	1:00 p.m.	2:00 p.m.	3:00 p.m.
13:00	1:00 p.m.	2:00 p.m.	3:00 p.m.	4:00 p.m.
14:00	2:00 p.m.	3:00 p.m.	4:00 p.m.	5:00 p.m.
15:00	3:00 p.m.	4:00 p.m.	5:00 p.m.	6:00 p.m.
16:00	4:00 p.m.	5:00 p.m.	6:00 p.m.	7:00 p.m.
17:00	5:00 p.m.	6:00 p.m.	7:00 p.m.	8:00 p.m.
18:00	6:00 p.m.	7:00 p.m.	8:00 p.m.	9:00 p.m.
19:00	7:00 p.m.	8:00 p.m.	9:00 p.m.	10:00 p.m.
20:00	8:00 p.m.	9:00 p.m.	10:00 p.m.	11:00 p.m.
21:00	9:00 p.m.	10:00 p.m.	11:00 p.m.	12:00 p.m.
22:00	10:00 p.m.	11:00 p.m.	12:00 p.m.	1:00 a.m.
23:00	11:00 p.m.	12:00 a.m.	1:00 a.m.	2:00 a.m.

For Dummies: Bestselling Book Series for Beginners

eBay® Bargain Shopping

FOR DUMMIES®

eBay® Bargain Shopping
FOR
DUMMIES®

Marsha Collier
Author of *Starting an eBay Business For Dummies*

WILEY

Wiley Publishing, Inc.

eBay® Bargain Shopping For Dummies®

Published by
Wiley Publishing, Inc.
909 Third Avenue
New York, NY 10022

www.wiley.com

WILEY   is a trademark of Wiley Publishing, Inc.

About the Author

Marsha Collier spends a good deal of time on eBay. She loves buying and selling (she's a Power Seller), as well as meeting eBay users from around the world. As a columnist, author of two best-selling books on eBay, and guest lecturer at eBay University, Marsha shares her knowledge of eBay with millions of online shoppers.

Out of college, Marsha worked in fashion advertising for the *Miami Herald*; then she worked as Special Projects Coordinator for the *Los Angeles Daily News*. Upon the birth of her daughter in 1984, she founded a home-based advertising and marketing business. Her successful business, the Collier Company, Inc., was featured by *Entrepreneur* magazine in 1985, and in 1990, Marsha's company received the Small Business of the Year award from her California State Assemblyman and the Northridge Chamber of Commerce.

More than anything, Marsha loves to get a great deal — that's what drew her to eBay in 1996 — and that's what keeps her busy at the site now. She buys everything from replacement toothbrush heads to parts for pool equipment to designer dresses. Marsha knows how to *work* eBay, and in this book she shares that knowledge with you.

Dedication

For my Mother, Claire Berg, who taught me how to shop for quality on a budget, and who I miss every day.

For my daughter Susan Dickman, who continues to help me perfect that talent.

Author's Acknowledgments

Thanks to my husband, Beryl Lockhart, and my daughter Susan, for putting up with the fact that eBay has taken over my life. I promise to take a day off soon. Also, thanks to the gang at Wiley: Andy Cummings (my unpretentious publisher); Steve Hayes, who's always there for me, and Nicole Haims, a darn good editor; without her expertise, this book wouldn't be as good.

Also, a big thanks to the eBay sellers that put up with my phone calls and inquiries; Patti "Louise" Ruby (aunt*patti), Steve Lindhorst (greenfuz), Wendy Warren (mrswarren), Shelly from Shoetime, and Rosalinda from the Auction Guild.

Publisher's Acknowledgments

We're proud of this book; please send us your comments through our online registration form located at www.dummies.com/register/.

Some of the people who helped bring this book to market include the following:

Acquisitions, Editorial, and Media Development

Project Editor: Nicole Haims

Senior Acquisitions Editor: Steven Hayes

Copy Editor: Nicole Haims

Technical Editor: Patti Louise Ruby

Editorial Manager: Carol Sheehan

Permissions Editor: Laura Moss

Media Development Manager:
Laura VanWinkle

Media Development Supervisor:
Richard Graves

Editorial Assistant: Amanda Foxworth

Cartoons: Rich Tennant
(www.the5thwave.com)

Cover Photo: ©Getty Images

Production

Project Coordinator: Erin Smith

Layout and Graphics: Amanda Carter, Lauren Goddard, LeAndra Hosier, Tiffany Muth

Proofreaders: Angel Perez, Charles Spencer, Kathy Simpson, Brian Walls, TECHBOOKS Production Services

Indexer: TECHBOOKS Production Services

Publishing and Editorial for Technology Dummies

    Richard Swadley, Vice President and Executive Group Publisher

    Andy Cummings, Vice President and Publisher

    Mary C. Corder, Editorial Director

Publishing for Consumer Dummies

    Diane Graves Steele, Vice President and Publisher

    Joyce Pepple, Acquisitions Director

Composition Services

    Gerry Fahey, Vice President of Production Services

    Debbie Stailey, Director of Composition Services

Contents at a Glance

Table of Contents

Introduction

*R*ecently I called a store to find out if it had a specific item in stock. "Oh yes," the sales clerk replied, "We have it, but we can't quote the price over the phone — you'll have to come into the store to find out the price."

So I went to the store. Not only didn't the store have what I was looking for, but the sales clerk tried to sell me a completely different product than the one I came in for. There is nothing worse than knowing that your time is being wasted.

I went back to my office, ran a search at eBay, ordered exactly what I needed — at 40 percent off the retail price — and it arrived in the mail three days later. I should have tried eBay first. eBay has become the world's online marketplace. It's mine now and it should be yours.

eBay found its way onto my computer in 1996, very early on. My daughter's hobby at the time was replacing her *She-Ra Princess of Power* action figures, which I had long previously sold at a garage sale. eBay saved my reputation as the mother who got rid of her collection. We replaced every figure with action figures that were MOC (that is, mint on card). I wasn't the only one shopping for action figures at eBay. In fact, the company attributes its initial growth to the Beanie Baby craze!

But as the eBay user base grew, savvy sellers tried to merchandise more than just collectibles. Today, eBay has gone past its status as an online auction house — it's now an international marketplace for everything, new and old. Famous manufacturers have their own outlets on the site, side by side the small mom-and-pop specialty boutiques.

I won't bore you with my entire shopping list, but as you can see, I've found a store that's open 24 hours a day, 7 days a week. You can afford to purchase things at eBay that you wouldn't ordinarily have the time to seek out or even afford in the bricks-and-mortar world.

About This Book

I've written this book so that you, too, can learn to take advantage of the megastore that is eBay. This book shows you how to get the bargains and stay safe in every major category of merchandise eBay offers.

Keep this book in your hands to help you feel at ease at eBay. I'd like to call it *eBay For Dummies Light,* but my publisher won't let me mess with the trademark. And really, it's not an accurate name. This book is just as packed with information as my larger *For Dummies* books, *eBay For Dummies,* 3rd Edition, and *Starting an eBay Business For Dummies.* The information in this book is simply targeted toward your interest in hunting for bargains.

There are great bargains to find, and down the road there's always the chance for you to sell some of the knick knacks that are collecting dust in your own closet. But the goal of this book is to help you reach your comfort zone to buy the things you want and need in your life, without dragging yourself all over town or spending wads of cash.

In this book, you'll find out

- ✔ How the eBay megastore (Web site) is laid out
- ✔ How to browse for your item by category and theme
- ✔ How to set up the search engine to sniff out the best deals
- ✔ What to look for when shopping for a particular item
- ✔ How to stay safe and protect your hard-earned money

Foolish Assumptions

If you've been intimidated by eBay in the past, your buying this book tells me a few things about you. First, I assume that you'd like to spend less time and money shopping for things that you'd like to own; second, I assume that you'd like to get in on all those bargains your neighbor keeps telling you he gets at eBay — but you don't want to make a career of buying and selling at eBay.

Here are some additional assumptions I've made:

- ✔ You have a computer with an Internet connection, or plan on getting one in the very near future.

- ✔ You are short on time and don't want to struggle through pages of techno-babble or dig around at the eBay Web site getting up to speed.

- ✔ You want to take your time and read this book at your leisure.

- ✔ You're nervous about possible fraud and want to know about the dangers of online shopping (without the hype) so that you can stay safe. To be forewarned is to be forearmed.

- ✔ You don't want to pay retail prices.

If you can say a resounding *yes!* to most of these assumptions, then this is the book for you. Read on!

How to Use This Book

This book is written so that you can read it in the fashion most comfortable to you. You can pick it up and read a bit, then put it down and pick it up again later. If you have a specific need or question, use the index or the Table of Contents to narrow down to just what you're looking for and go there.

This book is not written in *linear* style, which means that my editor double-checks to see that each chapter carries its own message; and you don't *have* to jump around; but if you want to, you can read Chapter 7, move on to Chapter 4, and skip ahead to Chapter 19, depending on your interests.

I do recommend that you read Chapter 1 before you get too far along so that you can find out what you need to know to become a registered eBay user.

How This Book Is Organized

Each part of this book covers an individual area of eBay. You should be able to find just what you're looking for in the specific chapters. If any task requires prior knowledge, I will point to the particular chapter where you will find the nuggets you need to know.

Part 1: Opening Up the Bargain-Filled World of eBay

In this part, I explain the basic layout of eBay — where to find what and how, and how to blast through the registration and bidding process. I also show you how to use eBay's online tools to keep your shopping organized.

You can find how to make your way through the site — and when you're through with this part, you should be comfortable with shopping at eBay.

Part II: Staying Safe While Shopping at eBay

Perhaps the reason you haven't added eBay to your shopping repertoire is because you've thought of eBay as a big scary place. You've read enough stories in the media about online transaction problems and you certainly don't want to become a victim of some notorious scammer. In this part, I show you how to stay safe and tell you what to do if you think you've got a problem.

In this part I also show you the safest ways to pay for your eBay purchases and protect your identity online.

Part III: Searching eBay

This section hones in on how eBay organizes the items for sale, and shows you how to cruise eBay's categories for something you didn't know you needed.

I'll teach you some special tricks (previously known only to geeks and eBay pros) to tweak eBay's search engine so you can locate the exact item you're looking for.

Part IV: Shopping for Specific Items

By wending your way through the eBay categories, you can do most of your shopping from the privacy of your own home. You won't believe some of the fun and unusual items that I've found at eBay. The chapters in this part reveal what a great place eBay is to shop; I guarantee that you will discover an item or two you never would have expected were for sale at eBay.

Part V: Specialty Shopping

One of the wonderful things about eBay is that it lets you shop your way. First, there are the specialty sites, such as Sothebys.com, which allow you to bid (or simply watch the auction action from the sidelines) in more high-stakes auctions. Also, if you like the products sold by a particular seller, find out whether the seller has his or her own store.

One of the best ways to shop your own way is to stay close to home. Of course, you could always buy that piano from 2,000 miles away (and pay for the shipping), but you might also check the Regional page to find out if there's a Steinway available in the next town over.

If you like browsing aisle after aisle of closeouts, then the online version of the bricks-and-mortar liquidation stores, provided by eBay, is right up your alley. Have fun, but be sure you read the fine print. I tell you everything you need to know in Chapter 17.

Part VI: Going for the Gold

eBay is far more than a collectibles auction venue these days. High-dollar items make up a large part of the daily transactions at eBay.

Did you know that more cars are sold at eBay than almost any-where else? Think about it. If you're looking for a special vintage car, or even a good reliable car to take you to work, you've got everything from certified pre-owned cars to brand-new cars straight from the dealers' lots to the cars that were only driven to church on Sundays by the little old lady down the way.

There's also a tremendous market in real estate — open land in Colorado; homes in North Carolina; timeshares in Florida.

Own your own piece of America from your armchair — right here at eBay. This part gives you tips on what to look for and tells you what questions to ask.

Fine jewelry has become de rigueur at eBay for the cognoscenti. (That means the smart folks are getting the good stuff at eBay for bargain basement prices!) I'll show you how to join them and know just how to find the deals.

Part VII: The Part of Tens

The Part of Tens is the most-fun part of an already very fun book.
I've listed my ten favorite reasons that shopping at eBay is fun.
And I asked several eBay sellers to advise new eBay bidders on the
things they need to know to be savvy bargain hunters at eBay.

Icons Used in This Book

 When you see this icon, check for information that shortens your
learning cycle. These tips enable you to bypass some of the more
onerous tasks and complete your goal in a more direct manner.

 Remember when Mom would wag her finger at you, while repeating
an oft-heard phrase, just to drive home an important truism? Same
thing here. Although I try not to be a nag, the important nuggets
you find in these icons are things you should not forget.

 This small icon signifies some piece of information that, ignored,
could get you into a bit of trouble. By following this warning
symbol, you'll stay on the side of safety.

Graphics and Screen Images

eBay is a graphically driven Web site. eBay programmers and product people work night and day tweaking and improving the site for
eBay users. In other words, sometimes what you see on-screen
may not match the screen images in the printed book. As hard as
my editor and I try, no printed book can ever keep up with the
sharp minds of this nimble crew.

Pages at eBay may change, but the philosophies in this book will
remain intact. Once you master the information in this book, no
matter what changes are made to the site, you will be able to
follow what's going on on-screen.

We've also made this book a convenient size so that you can tuck it
discreetly into your meeting notes or into your purse. That calls
for some creativity on our part so that we can show you only
what's worth seeing. I trimmed all evidence of the Internet browser
out of the on-screen images. You all know what your browser looks
like, so I won't bore you with details that aren't needed.

Where to Go from Here

The beginning is a very good place to start. If you're already registered at eBay, and are ready to jump in, find a spot in the book that
covers something new to you and start there.

Once you've got some of the basics under your belt, take your Web
browser to www.ebay.com and poke around. I highly recommend
poking around before actually buying something — you won't miss
the best bargain to come along in the century — there's always
another up at eBay!

Please visit my Web site, www.coolebaytools.com. (Cool eBay
Tools, get it?) See if there's some additional information there that
can help you. I always enjoy readers' comments and suggestions,
so you can also send e-mail to me from my site.

Happy shopping!

Part I

Opening Up the Bargain-Filled World of eBay

The 5th Wave   By Rich Tennant

"It's a Weber PalmPit Pro Handheld barbeque with a 24 btu, rechargeable battery pack, and applications for roasting, smoking, and open-flame cooking. Can you believe there was no reserve?"

In this part. . .

*P*art I of this book shows you how to use eBay tools to your best advantage. After reading these chapters, you'll no longer be intimidated by the eBay forms and pages. You'll also learn my deepest, darkest eBay shopping secrets. Apply these secrets to all the other tips in this book, and you may never have to drag yourself from store to store to buy something again.

Chapter 1

Getting Started at eBay

* *

* *

*P*erhaps you've actually visited the eBay Web site once or twice with the idea that you might buy something. Did you look for something simple like a *golf club?* Did eBay come up with several thousand listings? Or maybe you figured you'd get smart and narrow it down to a search for a *3 iron,* and you still got over a thousand listings? Yes, I understand, dear reader. The eBay site can be pretty daunting.

Maybe you started looking at listings and then got so scared that you'd get ripped off that you just left the site. Don't feel alone. When you're done reading this book, you'll have the information you need to be able to zip onto the site and find just what you're looking for, and to select the right seller to buy it from (at the best price, of course).

I like to shop from home, and eBay works much better for me than any quasi-convenient TV shopping channel because there's no overly-made-up huckster telling me how great I'd look in the outfit on the screen (worn by a size 4 model). On the eBay site, I have the opportunity to leisurely look the items over, read the descriptions and terms (in my own time), and click a link to ask the seller a question before I bid or buy. Using eBay is as simple as that. If I don't like the way a seller responds to my question, I can just go on to the next one. That's the great thing about eBay: There's always another seller and always another item for sale.

Nope, eBay Isn't a Store

If you speak to any of the employees at eBay, they will clearly tell you that eBay isn't a store; it's a *venue*. In the same way your high school gym was a venue when you went to dances, eBay is a venue for buyers and sellers. You had to follow the rules of the gym (and the school) or you were booted out without ceremony. It's the same way at eBay. Everyone has to follow the rules, or you can become a NARU (*Not A Registered User*) and banned from the site. (Yes, eBay really does ban users — for life.)

In reality, eBay is the world's largest online marketplace of goods and services, used by the world's largest community of individuals and businesses.

In the beginning days of eBay, people used to refer to the site as a giant online flea market or garage sale. But you can't call it that anymore. When you have mom-and-pop home operations (like mine) successfully doing business head to head with Martha Stewart, Sharper Image, and Ritz Camera (just to name a few), you've got something really unique. The coolest part for buyers is that anyone — from Martha Stewart to your next-door neighbor — has an equal chance to buy the same quality goods at a bargain price. It doesn't matter who you are when you shop at eBay — what matters is how you bid.

The eBay site really just gives sellers a great online home, a *community,* to sell their goods, and supplies them necessary tools for online trading in the auction-style and fixed-price selling formats. These sellers can reach all over the world and offer buyers things that they may never have been able to buy in their part of the country.

Community Values

When eBay originally came on to the Internet as Auction Web on Labor Day 1995, its founder, Pierre Omidyar, set up ethical guidelines for users of the system to follow. To this day, eBay follows an important credo of community values. Community values are so important to the company that every eBay employee is issued a copy of the values with his or her company ID security badge.

The eBay community is guided by these five fundamental values, which are posted on the Web site:

- ✔ We believe people are basically good.
- ✔ We believe everyone has something to contribute.

✔ We believe that an honest, open environment can bring out the best in people.

✔ We recognize and respect everyone as a unique individual.

✔ We encourage you to treat others the way you want to be treated.

When you register to bid or buy at eBay, you become a member of the eBay community and agree to follow these rules.

Okay, I can see you scoffers out there in the back row. We all know there are bad apples in every basket, and Part II of this book tells you how to steer clear of them and what to do if you ever cross paths with any of them. These are still good tenets to follow.

Find Just about Anything to Buy

Most of the first items sold at eBay were collectibles. Word of the early Web site spread like wildfire through Internet chat rooms and newsgroups. To be perfectly honest, many people really weren't quite convinced that selling online would become anything more than a hobby.

During the early days, I was selling Star Trek memorabilia at Auction Web, and doing quite well. I remember running into William Shatner (Captain Kirk of Star Trek fame) at a marketing meeting in mid-1997. Anxious to let him know how well I was doing with my merchandise online, I tried to explain Auction Web. Shatner scoffed, "No one will ever make any money on the Internet." (Really, I have witnesses — remember this is the future Mr. Priceline.com.) Ah, well.

Today, you can buy everything at eBay — and I mean almost anything you can imagine. eBay has over 18,000 categories and sub-categories of items. (When I wrote the first edition of *eBay For Dummies* in 1999, there were only 4,000 categories — and that seemed like a lot of categories back then!) You can buy brand new items, direct from a manufacturer or one of eBay's stores or you can buy slightly used goods. (Ever buy something at a sale, try it on once, and decide it didn't work for you?)

And there are always antiques, wholesale items, and unclaimed freight! Many stores sell their returns at eBay, perfectly good items in brand new condition that can't legally be sold again as new. Everything is here from fine art (Sotheby's is currently auctioning an original Rubens oil lamp with a starting bid of $1,000,000), a Gulfstream jet (sold for $4.9 million), land (your own private island in the Caribbean), to authentic antique furnishings, and more.

In this book, I take you all over the eBay site, and you'll be surprised at some of the things you'll find for sale! If you want to see some of the truly amazing items, browse the big ticket items area (Figure 1-1) at `http://pages.eBay.com/buy/bigticket/index.html`.

Things You Won't Find at eBay

Scruples are alive and well at eBay. You're forbidden from buying or selling certain things. Here's a list of some of the things you won't find on the site (you can find the entire list at `http://pages.ebay.com/help/community/png-items.html`):

✔ **Alcohol:** Unless the alcohol is in a collectible container, making the value of the container worth more than the contents, you can't buy hooch at the eBay site. But you may be able to purchase wine from a licensed wine broker who has been approved by eBay to sell spirits on the site. Oh yes, you still have to be 21 to purchase it.

Wine can only be sold by dealers who have been vetted by eBay as legally able to sell wine.

✔ **Animals:** No live animals may be sold, nor may any stuffed migratory birds. Pelts and parts of any animal that's an endangered species are also forbidden.

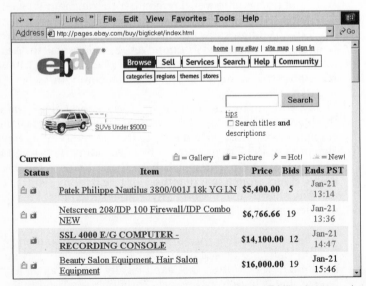

Figure 1-1: Better bring your credit card, or maybe a T-bill, when you shop here.

✔ **Fireworks:** The category of forbidden fireworks includes aerial bombs, booby traps (pull string), bottle rockets, chasers, daygo bombs, firecrackers, fountains, nitro poppers, party poppers, roman candles, skyrockets, smoke balls, smoke bombs, snap caps, snappers, sparklers, sparks, and torpedoes.

✔ **Human Parts and Remains:** Nope, you can't buy a kidney, sperm, or eggs at eBay. But if you'd like to purchase a real skull or skeleton for educational purposes, it's well within the rules.

✔ **Weapons:** No firearms, period. Not even if they are antique or collectible. No hand weapons, nunchaku, throwing stars, switchblades, or disguised knives.

✔ **Miscellaneous no-no's:** No counterfeit currency, credit cards, drugs and drug paraphernalia, or tobacco.

eBay understands that the community is made up of a diverse group of people. Offensive material is not tolerated on the site. If you're into auctions that promote hatred, violence, or intolerance, you're out of luck. Such items are "judiciously disallowed." You're also out of luck if you're interested in items that promote organizations (such as the KKK, Nazis, neo-Nazis, and Aryan Nation) with such views.

Please realize that I can't possibly give you a complete list of forbidden or questionable items. If you really want to investigate this subject thoroughly, for a current listing go to `http://pages.ebay.com/help/community/png-items.html`.

The eBay venue offers, of course, a very active Mature Audience category. You'll have to find it yourself because I don't have the space to cover it in the book. To enter the adult area (when you find it in the Everything Else category), you have to be a registered user of eBay with a valid credit card number on file — to verify that you're over 18 — and confirm agreement to the Mature Audience category Terms of Use.

Feeling at Home Online

Do you use your computer often? Do you visit Web sites on a regular basis? If so, I don't have to worry about you feeling at home online. If you only use your computer for e-mail, you're missing a whole world of exciting information.

How fast is Google?

After running a search on one of my book titles, Google comes up with 22,700 references that can be accessed with a click of my mouse. How long did this search take? Only .05 seconds.

Google is so fast and convenient that I hardly ever look at my recipe books anymore. When I want to know how to make something, I just type in the name of the recipe on Google, and I'm usually presented with a choice of many versions of the same item. I print it out (and save the recipe on my computer) and now I'm making my own recipe books!

Using search sites to find information about auction items

You can use the Internet to research and establish prices for all kinds of items, as well as keep you up on today's trends and fashions. Search engines, such as www.google.com, allow you to enter almost any search phrase or a group of keywords. After you enter the words that you would like more information on, a page appears with a long list of relevant Web sites that can answer questions about collectibles — and anything else you may have a question about.

If you're looking for price information about new items, check my Web site, www.coolebaytools.com, for links to some street price comparison sites for new items.

I also highly recommend John Levine, Carol Baroudi, and Margaret Levine Young's *The Internet For Dummies,* 8th Edition (Wiley Publishing, Inc.). I discovered quite a few tricks for successfully using Internet search engines in this well-written, funny, and enlightening book.

Getting set up

You're going to need several things to get started at eBay. The first is the need to acquire items. (Somehow I don't think this is going to be a problem.) In order of importance, here's the list:

   ✔ **Credit card or bank account:** Very important, as many sellers are kind of picky when it comes to getting paid for the items they sell to you. (For more information about paying for your purchases safely, see Chapter 8.)

✔ **Internet access:** A home Internet connection through a local ISP (Internet service provider) is the best, although many people only log on to the Internet from work. (If your company has policies against such frivolities, beware.)

✔ **Internet browser:** On your home computer, you will have an Internet browser. This is the software that enables you to browse the Internet. In this book (and on my home computer), I use Microsoft's Internet Explorer.

✔ **E-mail software:** When you browse eBay and find items that interest you, you may have questions for the seller. The seller will respond via e-mail. To read the responses, along with e-mail messages that eBay and other associated services like PayPal send you, you need e-mail software. Luckily, this also comes with your computer or is supplied by your ISP. I use Microsoft Outlook, which is part of the Office suite, but Outlook Express comes with almost every PC and does a great job for everyday e-mail. (If you use Web-based e-mail, see the sidebar titled, "Using Yahoo! or Hotmail? Grab your credit card," elsewhere in this chapter.)

✔ **eBay User ID:** Your ID is very important ! You've got to figure out a name to use for your user identification name at eBay. Think of a clever name that describes you or your hobbies. My User ID is *marsha_c*. It's not very creative (but then, I started at eBay in 1996, and it worked fine for me then). I'm afraid to change my ID now because no one would ever find me again!

Your eBay User ID has some rules. Your User ID must be at least two characters long, can't contain any spaces (but you can use the underscore (_) or the dash (-) within the name), it can't be obscene or profane, and it can't be a Web site or e-mail address. You also can't use "eBay" in your ID unless you are an employee of eBay. eBay doesn't allow the use of the symbols @, <, >, and &, and it also doesn't allow the use of the letter "e" followed by numbers. By the way, eBay User IDs can't be traded or sold.

Registering to Do Business at eBay

You can browse eBay all you want without registering, but before you transact any sort of business at eBay, you must register.

I recommend registering while you're reading this book. The moment you're armed with all this information, you'll be ready to go shopping and you won't want to miss even one bargain!

You can browse eBay without a User ID, but you can't place a single bid without being a registered member of the eBay community.

Here's what you need to do:

1. **Get yourself to the eBay home page at** www.ebay.com **(shown in Figure 1-2).**

   You see an area that says Welcome New Users. Within that area is a hyperlink box that beckons to you: Register Now.

2. **Ready? Go ahead, click that box!**

   After you click the Register Now hyperlink box, you'll come to the first of the registration pages, as shown in Figure 1-3. Notice two things when you get to this page:

   • At the top of the page, eBay tells you that by registering here you are also registering at Half.com (very convenient — for more about Half.com, flip to Chapter 17).

   • At the bottom of your browser window in the status bar on either the left- or right-side lower-right corner is a small padlock icon or a solid key icon that didn't appear before.

Click here to register.

Figure 1-2: Where the magic begins.

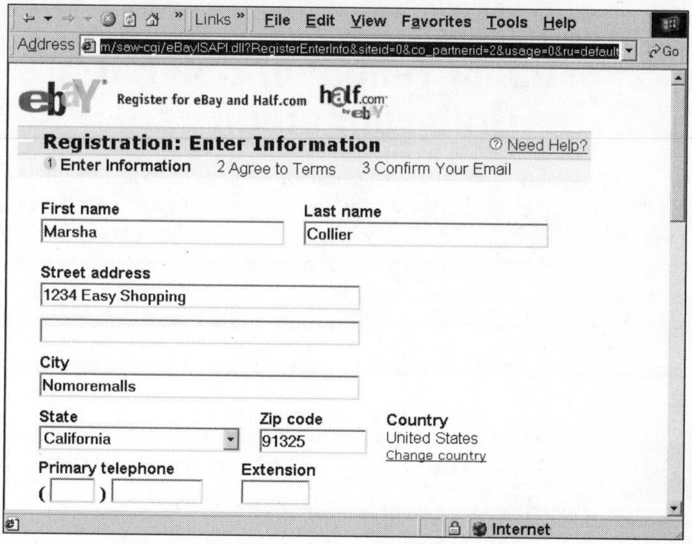

Figure 1-3: The first Secure Registration page.

The padlock icon means that eBay has moved you to a secure place on its site where no one else can see or receive your personal information. Your information is treated with the highest security, and you can fill out these forms with the utmost level of confidence.

3. Type your name, address, and telephone number.

Press the Tab key (or using the mouse to relocate your cursor) to move between text entry boxes.

This information is important if eBay ever needs to get in touch with you. Also, if you're involved in a transaction with another eBay member and he or she needs to get in touch with you, the other member can request your phone number as well as your city and state.

Don't fool around, like I did with my address in Figure 1-3. eBay's computers match zip codes and area codes and will catch errors!

4. Further down the page, you need to enter your e-mail address.

In fact, you have to type your e-mail address in two separate boxes so that eBay can be sure that you didn't mistype the address. It's critical to your registration. eBay will send you an e-mail with information you need to complete the process when you finish this page.

Using Yahoo! or Hotmail? Grab your credit card

Sellers must register at eBay with a credit or debit card to pay for their eBay fees; buyers do not. That is, unless they choose to use a free, Web-based e-mail account like those offered by Yahoo! or Hotmail. Most free e-mail services do not verify their users, so for the protection of all eBay users, eBay requires people with a free, Web-based e-mail account to register a credit card for identification purposes. Your credit card will not be charged.

It is safe to use your personal e-mail address for eBay registration. You will not be put on any e-mail lists.

5. **Enter your desired User ID.**

Don't strain your brain too much right now over your choice of User ID. If your chosen ID is taken, eBay has a cute little tool to help you select one. All you have to do is enter the information asked for (see Figure 1-4) and click the Suggest Some User IDs button.

If you find yourself unhappy with your initial choice, you can change it again next month. In fact, you can change your User ID once every 30 days if you like.

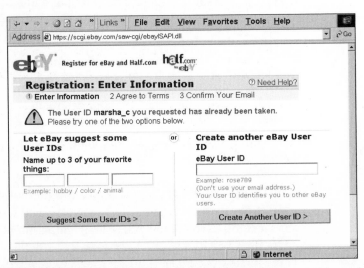

Figure 1-4: The eBay Instant User ID widget form.

When you change your User ID at eBay, an icon of a very suspicious looking pair of sunglasses appears next to your User ID. These shades stay with you for 30 days. There's nothing intrinsically wrong with the shades; however, double-check when you see a seller with a pair of these shades next to his or her name because the seller may have just changed his or her User ID to distract from a bad reputation. The good news is that users who change their IDs can't hide their reputations completely. You can find out the dirt on any eBay user by reading his or her feedback profile. (You can read more about feedback in Chapter 5.)

6. **Pick your password.**

The best passwords for eBay (or any Web site, for that matter) consist of over six characters and are a combination of letters and numbers. Never use your User ID as a password, your name, your pet's name, your address, or anything that may be easily known by others. C'mon, get a little cagey, you can do it. Get creative here.

7. **Select a secret question.**

The secret question is used to help you remember your password, should you forget it. There are six choices. I suggest that you select a question other than "What is your mother's maiden name?" because this question is often used by banks and financial institutions for identification purposes. Guard your mother's maiden name and don't give it out to anyone blithely.

8. **Supply your birth date.**

The people at eBay want this information for two reasons:

- They want to be sure that you are of legal age to do business at eBay.

- They want to send you e-mail wishing you a happy birthday!

9. **When you have completely filled out the entire form, click the Continue button.**

On the page that appears, you're asked to agree to eBay's User Agreement. Boil this agreement down to its basics, and the agreement says that you will play by the rules, that you know that every bid you place is a legally binding bid to buy, and so on.

I recommend you take a look at the rules. If you don't agree with them, you can't join the community. The rules are for everyone's protection.

You are also presented with the eBay Privacy Policy, which is one of the most comprehensive privacy policies I've ever seen on the Internet. eBay's commitment to protecting your privacy is another part of eBay's successful formula to keep its users happy and secure.

10. **Click to add a check mark in the box to assure you are over 18, and then click to add a check mark in the box that says that you know that you can choose to opt out of mailings from eBay.**

11. **After checking the two boxes, click the button that says I Agree To These Terms.**

    See Figure 1-5.

    After completing the registration, you can go to your My eBay page and change your notification preferences. (I show you how to do this in Chapter 4.)

    You're also notified that an e-mail message has been sent to the address you supplied during your registration.

12. **Open your e-mail program (if it isn't already open), and receive your e-mail.**

    When you open the message from eBay, the e-mail looks strikingly similar to the e-mail message shown in Figure 1-6.

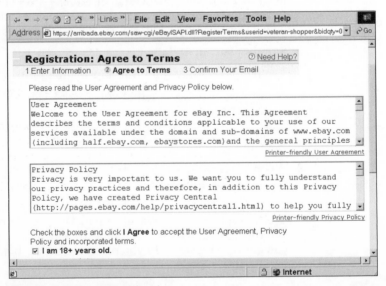

Figure 1-5: You're almost done!

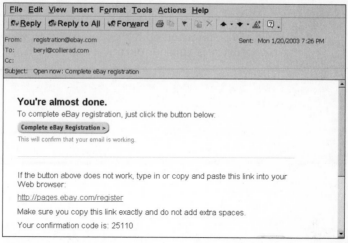

Figure 1-6: Registration e-mail.

13. **Follow the instructions on the e-mail. Click the button that says Complete eBay Registration.**

    If the link doesn't work, go to `http://pages.eBay.com/register` and enter the confirmation code that appears in your e-mail.

    In the very unlikely event that this e-mail does not reach you, go to `http://pages.eBay.com/services/registration/reqtemppass.html` and enter your e-mail address.

14. **Click the Submit button.**

    You will receive another e-mail with a special one-time confirmation password.

    After you reconnect with eBay through the Complete Registration button or by typing this URL into your Web browser, and you have submitted your registration code, a page that says `Congratulations, you are registered` appears. Welcome to the world's largest community of savvy shoppers! Now the fun begins.

Chapter 2

Bidding, Buying, and Winning

· ·

· ·

Although this book is loaded with fun and exciting eBay shopping tips, you don't have to finish reading it before you decide to log on and buy something. Here's the chapter where I take you through the paces of bidding, buying, winning, and finalizing your purchase.

Before you buy or bid, you need to understand how the different types of sales at eBay work, and how to take the best advantage of them.

Signing In

The first thing you need to do is sign in. I'm telling you this from personal experience. You can't do anything worthwhile at eBay without signing in. Usually, as soon as my browser hits the eBay site, I get excited about an item, but I can't bid on it because I'm not signed in. At times like these, signing in seems like a horrendous, tortuous task. So save yourself the trouble — sign in now. Click the <u>Sign In</u> link above the Navigation bar. The Sign In page, shown in Figure 2-1, appears.

You see a link on the page (indicated on Figure 2-1 by the hand shaped cursor) asking if you want to sign in via eBay's secure server. If you're the secure type, click the link, and you're redirected to eBay's secure server. (A small padlock or a key also appears in the lower-left or right corner of your browser window.)

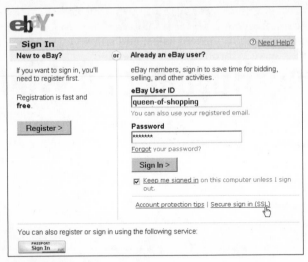

Figure 2-1: The eBay Sign In page.

Type your User ID, password, and if this computer is at home and solely for your own use, click in the box that says Keep Me Signed In on This Computer.

If there is a chance that someone else may use the computer, do *not* click in this box. If you do, eBay will keep your User ID and password active on that computer. This is not a good thing if you don't know the other people who might be using the computer; anyone else can start bidding on your account!

By the way, you also see a Sign In link on the bottom of the page for Microsoft Passport account holders. If you're not a Passport account holder, don't worry about this link; if you are, you may sign in here.

After you've signed in, you're presented with links to go to your My eBay page, the Sell Your Item page, or the Announcement Board. You're going shopping, so you can either click the eBay logo to go to the eBay home page, or on the search box in the Navigation Bar to start searching for the perfect item.

Getting Into the Action

You've just found the item you want. It's perfect — you want it, and you want it now. You have checked out the seller's feedback and you're ready to bid.

When this situation arises (and it will) your knowledge of eBay's sales formats becomes important. In this section, I go over the various instances and types of sales, and show you the ways to successfully make it through each of them.

Your bid on an eBay item is a legally binding contract. eBay treats every bid, other than bids on some real estate sales or incorrectly placed bids, as binding. If you win an auction and do not go through with your commitment by purchasing the item, the seller will file a Non-Paying Bidder notice about you. If you establish a history as a non-paying bidder at eBay (that is, you repeatedly back out of sales), you have a strong chance of getting suspended.

Understanding the value of an auction item

How much an item sells for depends on how many people see the item, and how badly other bidders want it. You may think of the *retail price* or *book value* as a standard for pricing; yet neither may be accurate when it comes to shopping at eBay. In fact, I always say there are three prices for everything:

- ✔ The price a retailer *charges* for an item at the store
- ✔ The price *everyone* says something is worth
- ✔ The price an item *actually* sells for at eBay

All auctions at eBay run from 3 to 10 days, and at the end of the auction, the highest bidder wins the item. There are a lot on nuances on how to finesse the bidding process (see Chapter 3), but before you get into all that, you should understand the basics of how the system works, so read on.

Getting into the auction frame of mind

To give you a real-world sense of the auction process, here's a real-world example of my chocoholism put to the eBay test. I've found an item that I want, an order of homemade chocolate truffle bars. After reading the seller's feedback (and skipping lunch), I want them even more!

Not one of this seller's previous buyers was unhappy with the product. As a matter of fact, no one seems able to say enough about the quality of this candy. Yum! If it's really good, I can always buy more later and send them to partners as holiday gifts. (That'll make my shopping a tax write-off, no?)

As you look at the auction (shown in Figure 2-2), observe several things. The starting bid is $9.95, and the auction ends in over four days.

Artistic Hand Painted Chocolate Truffle Bars			
Item # 2312460488			
Home:Food & Wine:Candy, Chocolate:Other			

Current bid	US $9.95	Starting bid	US $9.95
Quantity	1	# of bids	0 Bid history
Time left	**4 days, 16 hours +**	Location	San Francisco, CA
		Country/Region	United States /San Francisco
Started	Mar-12-03 09:51:35 PST	✉	Mail this auction to a friend
Ends	Mar-17-03 09:51:35 PST	🔭	Watch this item
Seller (rating)	rejinsf (40) ☆		
	Feedback rating: **40** with 100% positive feedback reviews (Read all reviews)		
	Member since: May-29-01. Registered in United States		
	View seller's other items	Ask seller a question	🛡 Safe Trading Tips		

Figure 2-2: Something I really want to win.

You have several directions you can go in at this point. I have observed that auctions of this type of merchandise have a very active bidding pattern, so at this early stage I would suggest bidding the minimum amount just to get the item to show up as one of the items I'm bidding and watching from the My eBay page.

Bidding can often be like a game of poker; if you really want to win a one-of-a-kind item, don't show your hand to other bidders. Simply mark the auction to Watch. See Chapter 4 for instructions on how to *watch* an auction. However, for an item like this, which I'm sure will show up at eBay again, I wouldn't play my cards so close to my chest.

When it comes to auctions, the highest bid wins. *Remember this please.* People are constantly boo-hooing because they've been outbid at the last minute (or *sniped,* as I explain in Chapter 3). You can't be outbid if you are the high bidder!

If you're interested in an item but you don't have the time to follow it closely from the beginning of the auction to its conclusion, you can place a *proxy bid.* See the following section, aptly called "Proxy bidding," for more information.

Proxy bidding

Bidding at eBay goes up by pre-prescribed increments. But what if you're not able to sit in on an auction 24 hours a day, 7 days a week, upping your bid every time someone bids against you? (You mean you have a life?)

You do receive e-mail messages from eBay to let you know that you've been outbid, but experienced eBay buyers will tell you that waiting for an outbid notice (especially on an item you really want) is courting danger. The computers at eBay are often busy doing other things, and you might not get the notice in time to place a new competitive bid.

Enter eBay's proxy bidding system. *Proxy bidding* is the perfect way to place your bid for the highest amount you are willing to pay for an item — without wasting your valuable time.

Before you place your proxy bid, you should give serious thought to how much you want to pay for the item. Look at Table 2-1 for eBay's actual bidding increments.

Table 2-1	eBay's Bidding Increments
Current High Bid	*Next Bid Increased By*
$.01 to 0.99	$.05
$1.00 to 4.99	$.25
$5.00 to 24.99	$.50
$25.00 to 99.99	$1
$100.00 to 249.99	$2.50
$250 to 499.99	$5
$500 to 999.99	$10
$1,000 to $2,499.99	$25
$2,500 to 4,999.99	$50
$5,000 and up	$100

When you place a proxy bid at eBay, eBay's bidding engine submits a bid that's high enough to *barely* outbid the current high bidder. If the auction has no other bidders, your bid will appear as the minimum auction bid until someone bids against you, and is increased incrementally in response to other bids against yours.

No other eBay members know how much your proxy bid is.

Placing a bid

To place a proxy bid in an auction, scroll to the bottom of the page, and type in your maximum bid, and click the Place Bid button, as shown in Figure 2-3.

If the seller has set a Buy It Now price, and you're too impatient to wait until the end of the auction to win, click Buy It Now.

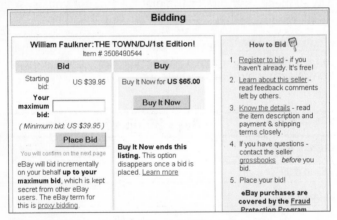

Figure 2-3: Enter your high bid or click Buy It Now.

A confirmation page appears, as shown in Figure 2-4.

You have one last chance to back out. If everything is in order, click either Buy It Now or Confirm Bid (depending on the type of transaction). Your transaction is not placed until you do this. If you get cold feet, click Back to Item. To find out more about the Buy It Now option, see "Buying Your Item Outright," later in this chapter.

The next page, shown in Figure 2-5, lets you know whether you're the high bidder (or whether your purchase has been confirmed if you decided to Buy It Now).

If you're not the high bidder in an auction, just scroll down the acknowledgement page to the rebidding square and place another bid.

Figure 2-4: Confirm your bid.

Congratulations! Your purchase has been confirmed.
CARE BEARS WASTE PAPER BASKET TRASH CAN M341 (Item #3213086977)

marsha_c, please review the seller's payment instructions below. You should contact your seller within 3 business days.

Seller's eBay ID: _____ (42517) ✦
Seller's Email: _____

Payment Details	Payment Instructions
Item price $14.94*	Please read the auction terms regarding
*Not including any shipping charges	the use of eBay Checkout

Figure 2-5: You just bought it now!

Understanding reserve prices

You'll often come across auctions, like the one in Figure 2-6, that have the words `Reserve has not been met` next to the bid amount. This means that the seller has protected his outlay in the item by placing a reserve on the bidding. By placing a reserve on the auction, the seller ensures that the item will not sell until the bidding reaches the mysterious reserve figure.

To save yourself time and trouble, if you're really interested in an item with a reserve, e-mail the seller and politely ask him (or her) how much the reserve is. Some sellers guard the reserve amount like the crown jewels, and other sellers will graciously reveal the figure. The point of the reserve is to protect their investment and get qualified bidders, not waste your time.

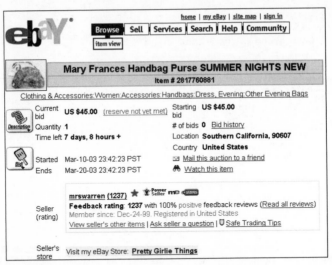

Figure 2-6: A reserve price auction for a lovely purse.

Private auctions

Private auctions are handled exactly the same way as plain-vanilla auctions, except for the fact that no one other than the buyer and the seller knows who the winner is. As a matter of fact, all bidders' names are hidden from investigation from anyone not bidding in the transaction.

After you've been at eBay a while, you'll see the same group of bidders bidding in the same auctions as you, you'll have similar tastes. Private auctions are very handy for snaring items secretly without your regular competitor knowing that you're bidding on the item (see Chapter 3 for bidding strategies).

Dutch auctions

A Dutch auction allows a seller to auction off multiple identical items (see Figure 2-7). You can bid on one or as many of the items as you wish. When the total number of items has been bid upon at the opening price, the next bids will have to beat the previous bids by one bidding increment.

When the auction is over, all winning bidders (those with the highest bids) win their items at the lowest bid price. I know that sounds ridiculous, but that's the way it works. I'm only reporting this — it must have taken a very creative mind to come up with this theory of auctions. If you want a more in-depth description of the Dutch process, go to http://pages.ebay.com/help/buy/buyer-multiple.html.

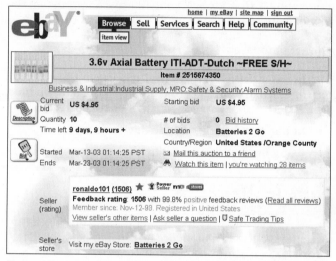

Figure 2-7: A Dutch auction for some really hard-to-find batteries for my alarm system.

To place a bid in a Dutch auction, you must input the amount of items you want to bid on and the amount you wish to bid per item, as shown in Figure 2-8.

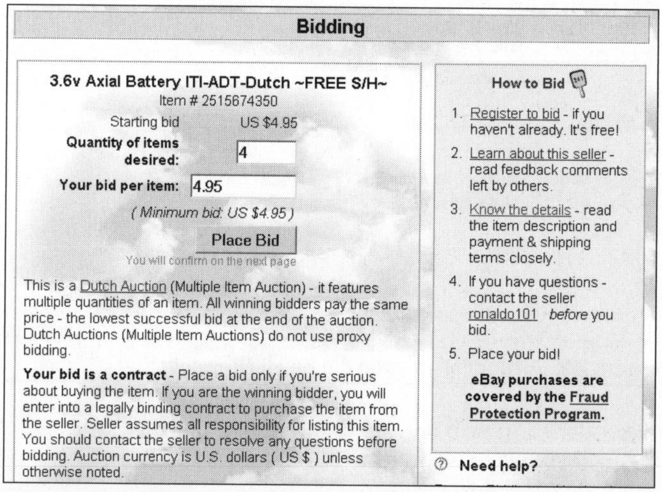

Figure 2-8: Bidding for 4 of the 10 items in a Dutch auction.

Buying Your Item Outright

Although eBay's success was built on auctions, the eBay company philosophy is that for everyone to grow and prosper, the auction venue ought to branch out and allow sellers to handle outright sales. There are three ways to buy outright at eBay. You can make a direct purchase

✔ **In one of eBay's stores (as I discuss in Chapter 16).** Stores offer exclusive items that aren't on the auction block. All items in stores are for sale at a posted price.

✔ **In fixed price sales on the auction site.**

✔ **Using the Buy It Now feature.**

Buy It Now

You may have already looked at auctions and sees a Buy It Now price next to the minimum or starting bid amount. That little indicator means that if you want the item badly enough, and the Buy It Now price is within your budget for the item, you can end the auction right then and there by buying the item for that amount. Take a look at Figure 2-9 to see what I mean.

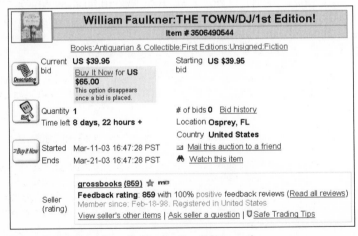

Figure 2-9: An auction offering the Buy It Now option.

Before using the Buy It Now option (because you think you've hit upon a bargain) be sure to check the seller's shipping charges. Many sellers set a low Buy It Now price, but place a high shipping amount on the item to make up their missing profits. If the shipping amount isn't listed, be sure to e-mail the seller and ask for the shipping amount. A Buy It Now transaction is *final,* and you can't withdraw your bid to buy.

If you decide that you want to buy, scroll down to the bottom of the page and click the Buy It Now button. An eBay confirmation page appears, and if you still want to make the purchase, you can confirm the purchase price. Then all you have to do is go through the checkout process and pay the seller.

If you come across an auction with the Buy It Now option, you can still place a bid. When a bid is placed on a Buy It Now item that has no reserve, the option to immediately buy disappears, and the item goes into strict auction mode. If the item has a reserve, the Buy It Now option disappears when the reserve is met.

Fixed-price sales

You may often come across items for sale at eBay without the option to bid. These are fixed-price listings and may be for a single item or for multiple items. You can buy as many as you like.

Yikes! 1 Made a Mistake!

We're all human and we make mistakes. Luckily for everyone, eBay members are allowed to retract bids under certain extreme circumstances.

You may retract your bid if you meet one of the following criteria:

- **You accidentally typed in the wrong bid amount:** Say you typed $900 and you meant $9.00. Oops. In a case like this, you can retract the bid, but you'd better rebid the proper amount (that original $9.00) immediately, or you may be in violation of eBay's policies.

- **The seller has added information to the item description that changes the value of the item considerably:** The bull that was let loose in the seller's shop has changed the mint condition of the Ming vase you just bid on? No problem.

✔ **You can't reach the seller through eBay's e-mail or through the telephone number you got from eBay's find members area:** Seller gone AWOL and you have a question about an item you've bid on? You can use eBay's e-mail system by clicking the <u>Ask the Seller a Question</u> link in the seller's box on the auction page.

Every time you retract a bid, it will appear on your eBay ID card on your feedback area.

Here are a couple of additional bid retraction restrictions:

✔ **You can only retract a bid if it was placed prior to the last 12 hours of an auction:** If you bid more than once in the last 12 hours of the same auction, only your last bid will be retracted.

✔ **When you retract a bid because of a bidding error, you wipe out any and all of your previous bids in the auction and you must bid again immediately to reinstate yourself as a bidder:** If you must retract your bid within the last 12 hours, you must send an e-mail to the seller asking him or her to cancel your bid. It is totally up to the seller whether to cancel your bid.

✔ **A bid retraction isn't a guarantee that you will get out of purchasing the item:** Sometimes, sellers simply don't have the opportunity or time to cancel a bid. That means you have to buy the item.

eBay vigorously investigates members who abuse bid retractions. Too many bid retractions and you may find yourself suspended from the system.

You'll probably never need this link, but to retract your bid (or find more information), go to `http://cgi.ebay.com/aw-cgi/eBayISAPI.dll?RetractBidShow`.

Got a question? Let your fingers do the, um, typing

To get the seller's telephone number go to the Search area, click <u>Find Members</u>, and input your transaction number and the seller's User ID. The good people at eBay will check to be sure that you've begun a transaction with this person, you'll get the seller's telephone number via e-mail to your registered e-mail address. Your phone number will also be e-mailed to the seller.

Winning the Auction and Checking Out

After you win the auction, or buy an item in a Buy It Now or fixed-price transaction, it's convenient to be able to pay directly and immediately. If it's after you've won, you can go back to the item and see a <u>Check Out</u> link on the item page.

Many sellers use off-site services to process payments like AuctionWorks or Channel Advisor. These services are very common and safe. Check out Chapter 8 for information on how to pay safely.

Chapter 3

Bargain Shopping Secrets *Exposed!*

. . . .

In This Chapter

▶ Timing your bid

▶ Shopping the competition's cart

▶ Winning bidding strategies

▶ Knowing what you're buying

. . . .

*I*f everyone likes a bargain, then I'm not like everyone — I *love* bargains! When I was teaching classes at eBay's own eBay University (yes, there really is one), my favorite class to teach was Buying and Browsing, because I love the thrill of the chase and the acquisition of a good deal without all the haggling.

Often, the first thing that people ask me is how they can stop getting outbid at the last minute of an auction. I always say the same thing — become an expert *sniper* and bid higher than the other guy!

Okay, but how? In this chapter I give you all my tips — including a few I picked up from other wise shoppers along the way.

The Secret's in the Timing

A bricks-and-mortar auction (remember those?), such as those held by Sotheby's or Christie's, ends when the bidding ends. No auctioneer is going to cut off the bidding for that one-of-a-kind Van Gogh, right? As long as someone is bidding, all systems are go. The last bidder standing wins.

But at eBay, things are different. Timing is important. The auctions at eBay close at a pre-prescribed time. Because of this fundamental difference in the way eBay runs its auctions, you need to do some special work to make sure that you can make the most strategically timed bid possible.

You can find out what time an auction ends by simply looking at the auction page.

Setting Your Computer to eBay Time

One of the first things you need to know is that eBay runs on Pacific Standard Time and that uses a 24-hour clock (it runs in military mode — 0:00 to 24:00 versus the more familiar 1:00 to 12:00).

To get the serious deals, you need to synchronize your computer's clock with eBay's. To find out what eBay's official time is, go to `http://cgi3.ebay.com/aw-cgi/eBayISAPI.dll?TimeShow`.

When you know eBay's official time, you need to compare it to your own computer's clock. On most Windows-based computers, the time is in the lower-right corner of the screen on the task bar.

Playing "Going, Going, Gone"

Although many people list their auctions to end at all hours of the day and night, it's only fair to say that the amount of bidders out in cyberspace is higher during certain hours. Between the hours of 23:00 (that's 11 p.m., Pacific Standard Time) and 03:00 (that's 3 a.m., Pacific Standard Time), things run a bit slowly at eBay. If you're online at that time, you may be able to take advantage of some very serious bargains. So swallow a shot of espresso and have fun if you're a night owl.

Going, Going, Gone is the name of the game my daughter and I used to play when we wanted to go shopping for fun at eBay. Visit your favorite eBay category and have fun. (If you're unfamiliar with categories, skip over to Chapter 11.)

You can choose to view the auctions that are going to end in the next five hours. This category sorting method is called, not coincidentally, Going, Going, Gone. Here you can cruise the auction closing while the world is asleep, and bid to your heart's content to get some great bargains.

To change the time on your computer's clock, follow these steps:

1. **Open your Internet browser and visit** `http://cgi3.`
   `ebay.com/aw-cgi/eBayISAPI.dll?TimeShow.`

   The official clock at the eBay Mother Ship appears, in the
   form of the Official Time page. Keep the browser open.

2. **Right-click on your computer's taskbar.**

   A context menu appears.

3. **Select Adjust Date/Time.**

   The Date/Time Properties window appears.

4. **Click the Internet browser to activate it, and then click
   the browser's Refresh button.**

   The page refreshes.

5. **Type the official eBay time into your computer's clock
   and click OK.**

Shopping Your Neighbor's Cart

When you have shopped eBay for a while, you will know the User
IDs of many of the people you bid against in auctions. Don't be surprised that there are other people in the eBay universe that have
the same quirky interests as you. You may even come to dislike
them if they outbid you often enough. It's a wretched feeling, being
outbid — especially when it happens at the last minute.

I remember once hearing a comedy routine about how much
quicker it is to shop in a supermarket from other people's
carts — and eBay is no different. When you've gotten to know
the IDs of your bidding competition, you can run bidder searches
on them.

For example, say *oldmeany123* outbids you in an auction for rare
antique glockenspiels, you can run a bidder search on the bidder
and find out what else he or she has been bidding on lately.

You can find out the following information when you run a bidder
search:

  ✓ **The items the bidder tends to be interested in:** Let your
    competition do the legwork of finding the items you like.

✔ **What time of day the bidder likes to make bids:** You can get a sense of whether the bidder is in another part of the country (or the world) and use the time difference to your advantage.

✔ **Other bidding habits:** Some bidders like to place an initial bid at the beginning of the auction and then swoop in at the end and snipe. Or they never bid until the end of the auction. Or, they never snipe. No matter what strategy your competition chooses, you can come up with a counter strategy to improve your likelihood of winning.

✔ **How high the bidder tends to like to bid:** This is a key to winning the auction by as few pennies as possible. Does the bidder end his or her bids with .27? End yours with .32. Also, if the other bidder is accumulating several similar items one at a time, you really have a good picture of *exactly* how much he or she will bid in this auction. Information is power!

This is not snooping! It's totally legal and acceptable. When you've checked out your competition's shopping cart, you can swoop in and bid or snipe back if you like the other items this bidder is interested in. Isn't it easier to let someone else do the legwork and find the bargains for you?

You can run a bidder search by doing the following:

1. **On the eBay Navigation Bar, click Search.**

2. **Click the By Bidder tab.**

3. **Enter the User ID of the bidder you want to check out.**

4. **Click the Search button.**

5. **To check the bidder's previous auctions, click in the Include Completed Items box.**

   You can see how high the bidder is willing to bid on certain items. This is invaluable information if you want to get a drift of how high *you* have to bid to win the next auction where you come into competition with your bidding nemesis.

You'll also see whether the bidder tends to snipe, or likes to bid at the beginning of the auction. Check the times of day the bidder likes to place bids; if the bidder is on the East coast and you're on the west, you may win some items while he or she is sleeping.

You may find that relying on the bidder search can give you a false sense of knowledge and confidence. Others may use the bidder search to become familiar with your habits, too. And many savvy buyers have two eBay User IDs and alternate back and forth to confuse those who try to follow their bidding patterns. Sniping can help because last-minute bidding doesn't reveal your hand until it's too late for other bidders to respond. No one will know you're interested in that giant teddy bear until you win it. Mix your bidding patterns up a bit — keep the competition wondering!

My Favorite Bidding Strategies

There used to be a time when I would tell beginning eBay members my favorite methods of bidding and winning, and if there was an eBay employee in earshot, you could see him or her wince as in pain. Things are considerably different these days.

For example, eBay used to officially oppose the use of third-party payment options — until eBay purchased PayPal. And sniping. Don't get me started. When sniping swept the online auction community, the eBay Powers That Be couldn't endorse the practice. Finally, after some agonizing, the eBay insiders admit that sniping *does* work in winning auctions.

As a matter of fact, eBay's instructors are now pitching many of the strategies that I've been pitching for years — because they work! While editing this book, my editor even reminisced about how much the official eBay party line has changed since we first worked together in 1999.

Hunting for errors

I have gotten some of my best buys at eBay by searching for misspellings. As a matter of fact, I keep a couple of searches for misspelled items on my own My eBay page. Many sellers are often in a hurry when they set up their auction listings, and to err is human. (To win, divine). Of course, there are also a good many sellers who just don't pay attention. I am more than willing to forgive sellers for their mistakes because the payoff for bargain hunters is, well, a *bargain.*

Think of alternate spellings when you search for an item. A favorite of mine is *Van Furstenberg* for *Von Furstenburg* (Diane, the designer, that is). Usually, I search for the correct spelling and find a bunch of items where the bidding can get steep. But when I search for the misspelled version of her name, I may find identical items, except the misspelled items don't have any bids, because I'm the only one who has found the listing.

You can be sure to cover a complete version of your search by searching using the tricks I outline in Chapter 10, looking for either word in a search *(furstenberg, furstenburg)*.

I was also very successful during the holiday season of 2002, when those computer-animated cats were popular (and going for extremely high prices at eBay, because they were sold out everywhere across the country). The brand name was FurReal. So I searched for spellings like *fur real* and *furreal.* You can find many bargains by searching for misspelled brand names.

Use asterisks as *wild cards* in your search, as well, especially if you're not sure of the spelling of a word. You can also find some nuggets when searching for the plural of an item. (Looking for a truckload of glockenspiels? Tack an *s* at the end of *glockenspiel!*) Check out Chapter 10.

Checking out the high bidder

Take a look at the high bidder in an auction that interests you. Does he or she have a lot of positive feedback? If he or she does, you can bet the farm that the bidder knows the ropes and may jump back in at the last minute with a winning bid.

A little sleuthing can go a long way when trying to beat the competition for a very special item. Open a bidder's feedback file and click the links to the auctions. Read the specific feedback messages for these auctions to get clues about the bidder's bidding style. When you get to the auction, double-click the bidding histories to get an idea of the time of day that the bidder wins. (If she is also a seller, you can look at her current and past auctions to get an idea of her time zone, too.)

Researching your item

Sometimes we (we, that's me *and* you) find what we think is an incredible deal at eBay. It well may be, especially if we know that the retail price is, say, $80, and we're seeing a Buy It Now, or an auction closing at $40. If a low, low price works for you — just go ahead and buy the item if you want it right away. To find the best price for any item at eBay, do your homework to find out what similar items at eBay tend to sell for.

When you conduct your eBay research, the best strategy is to look at the prices achieved in previous sales. Do a search for completed auctions and check these auctions' bid history. Click the <u>Bid History</u> link on the auction item page. (The link appears just next to the number of bids), and you'll be presented with the screen pictured in Figure 3-1.

Quick bidding tips

You can get your tips from many places, but when you get a tip — double-check who it's coming from. Visit eBay's Community boards and chats, and listen to what the others have to say. Before taking anything to heart, and changing the way you do things, check the tip-giver's experience. Is Miss Busy Body really experienced at eBay or is she just touting the current company line? Or even passing on the latest misinformation/gossip on the site? I often say I love buying from eBay sellers who are also buyers because they respect and understand what it's like to be a buyer at eBay!

---

eBay Bid History for
NEW Nicole Miller CIGAR 60" GOLF Umbrella (Item # <u>1047677651</u>)

Currently	$12.50	First bid	$9.99
Quantity	1	# of bids	2
Time left	Auction has ended.		
Started	Dec-12-01 10:03:32 PST		
Ends	Dec-17-01 10:03:32 PST		
Seller (Rating)	(1236) ★ me		

<u>View page with email addresses</u> (Accessible by Seller only) <u>Learn more.</u>

Bidding History (Highest bids first)

User ID	Bid Amount	Date of Bid
(113) ★	$12.50	Dec-17-01 09:32:07 PST
(6014) ☆ me	$12.00	Dec-12-01 17:43:20 PST

Remember that earlier bids of the same amount take precedence.

<u>Bid Retraction</u> and <u>Cancellation</u> History
There are no bid retractions or cancellations.

Figure 3-1: The bidding history lets you know what time bidders place their bids, and what the highest losing bid was.

Here are a few short tips that I know really work:

✔ **Shop eBay.ca, eh?** That's right. If you're in the United States, why not bid on auctions at the eBay Canada Web site? In fact, if you're an international bidder, and you're willing to pay shipping from the United States, then you'll have no problem handling Canadian shipping charges.

If you're an American resident, all you have to do is think about the conversion between the U.S. dollar and the Canadian, and oh, oh yes — there are bargains to be had. From the eBay home page, scroll down the left side of the page and click the <u>Canada</u> link. Or you can visit www.eBay.ca. Be sure the seller has reasonable shipping to the United States *before* you bid.

✔ **Place your bids in odd figures.** Many eBay bidders place their bids in the round numbers that match eBay's proxy system. You can win by a few cents if you place your bids in odd numbers like $10.97 or $103.01.

If two people bid the exact same amount at the end of an auction, the earliest bid (according to eBay's clock) wins. But if you and another bidder bid at just about the same time, you could win by a couple of pennies. I've done it many times. For example, a bid of $23.78 beats a bid of $23.75.

✔ **Don't get carried away in a bidding war.** Unless the item is *extremely* rare, odds are that a similar item will show up at eBay again someday soon. Don't let your ego get in the way of smart bidding. Let your opposition pay too much!

✔ **Watch for item re-listings.** If you see an item that you want, but it has too high an opening bid (or too high a reserve) for you to justify placing a bid, there's a good chance that no one else will bid on the item either. Put that auction into your Watch area of My eBay, and every so often after the auction ends, double-check the seller's auctions to see if the seller has re-listed the item with a lower starting bid and a lower (or no) reserve.

✔ **Combine shipping when possible.** When you purchase an item, double-check the seller's other auctions and see whether you're interested in making a second purchase. If you see something else that appeals to you, e-mail the seller to see if he will combine the items in shipping. That way you can make two purchases for a smaller single shipping bill. See Chapter 21 for more information about making multiple purchases.

✔ **Never bid early, but if you do, bid high.** The only time this bidding early works is if no one else is interested in the auction. Usually, though, the tactic will gear up another eBay user to outbid you because suddenly the item is valuable to at least one person. If you *must* bid before the auction's close, bid high. As a matter of fact, bid a couple of dollars more than you might want to pay. (I mean literally a couple, not a couple hundred.)

✔ **Try for a Second Chance offer.** If you get outbid and miss the chance to increase your bid on an auction item, you'd be smart to e-mail the seller and ask if he or she has any more. You may get lucky, and the seller can send you a Second Chance offer for your high bid.

A seller may send a Second Chance offer to any bidder who isn't the winning bidder under two circumstances:

- The winner does not go through with the winning bid.

- The seller has more than one of the item that was sold.

It is eBay-legal to purchase in this way. Any purchase you make in this manner will be covered under eBay's insurance, and you will have the opportunity to leave feedback.

Succeeding by Sniping

Sniping is my number one favorite way to win an auction at eBay. *Sniping* is the fine art of outbidding your competition in the very last seconds of the auction — without leaving them enough time to place a defensive bid. When I first touted this method in 1999, it was a fairly new idea. Now everyone knows about sniping, and it's pretty much an accepted bidding method.

Bidders (that is, losing bidders) whine and moan when they lose to a sniper — but there is one thing to remember. eBay uses proxy bidding. If you're going to snipe, always assume that the current bidder has a very high dollar proxy bid in the works. The high bidder always wins!

Sniping techniques for the beginner

Before you start sniping, be sure you know how fast your Internet connection will react. Figure out how long it takes to get your bid confirmed at eBay. Test it a few times until you know how many seconds you have to spare when placing a bid.

Also be sure you're signed in first, before you attempt a snipe.

Follow these steps to snipe at the end of the auction:

1. **In the last couple of minutes of the auction, locate the item you want to win and press the Ctrl key and the N key together to open a second window on your Internet browser.**

   Keep one window open for bidding.

2. **Continuously click the Reload or Refresh button in the browser toolbar.**

   By reloading the item continually, you'll be aware when you're in the last 60 seconds of bidding. You also can see instantly whether anyone else is doing any last-minute bidding.

3. **Type your maximum bid in the bid box of the second browser.**

   This is the highest amount you will consider paying for the item.

4. **Click the Place Bid button.**

   When you click the Confirm Bid button that appears on the next page, your bid is finalized.

5. **Do not press the Confirm Bid button yet.**

6. **Continuously refresh your first browser.**

7. **As the auction nears its end, confirm your final bid by clicking the Confirm Bid button.**

   The longer you can hold off to bid before the auction ends, the better.

The three-screen approach to sniping

If you really want an item badly enough, try setting up a back-up sniping setup. Try my three-screen system (see Figure 3-2). With the triple-screen system, you can place a back-up high bid in case you catch another sniper swooping in on your item immediately after your first snipe.

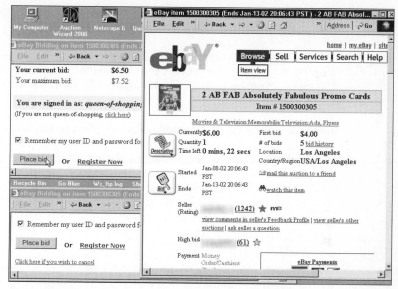

Figure 3-2: My three-browser sniping system in action.

Obviously, if you win with the first snipe — the second window is unnecessary. But if you lose the first one, that second window feels like a real life-saver! If you're outbid after two snipes, don't cry. The winner paid way more than you were willing to pay. It's not *much* consolation, but rarely is an item so rare that you only see it come on the auction block once in a lifetime. You'll have your chance again, I promise.

Mechanizing the Sniping Process

My daughter says that I can make almost anything I do high main-tenance, and that very well may be true. When it comes to eBay bidding and winning, there are a bunch of software programs and Web sites that can help automate your shopping and feedback process.

Auto-sniping your auctions

There are many reasons for not wanting to snipe your own auc-tions. You might not have the time to be there for the closing of each one, you may have a slow Internet connection, or you may just not want to bother. All are very valid reasons!

There are many companies out there who can help you in your sniping needs. Just remember that if you use software downloaded to your computer, your computer has to be online at the time of the auction.

Here are a few that I have used both of these programs successfully:

- ✔ **BidRobot:** BidRobot, shown in Figure 3-3, deftly places sniping bids for you from its servers. I admit to using BidRobot, and it's won many an auction for me while I've been on the road or busy writing. The service is one of the least expensive ones out there. It charges a low flat rate for all the snipes you could use. Get a free trial at www.bidrobot.com. Just enter the code *cool* in the registration box.

- ✔ **eSnipe:** Another very popular sniping server is eSnipe, shown in Figure 3-4. This service charges a fee of approximately 1 percent of the final winning price, with a maximum of $10 (you pay only if you win). You can purchase *Bid Points* to place in your account to pay for upcoming snipes. For 14 days of free sniping, use this link www.esnipe.com/marshacollier.

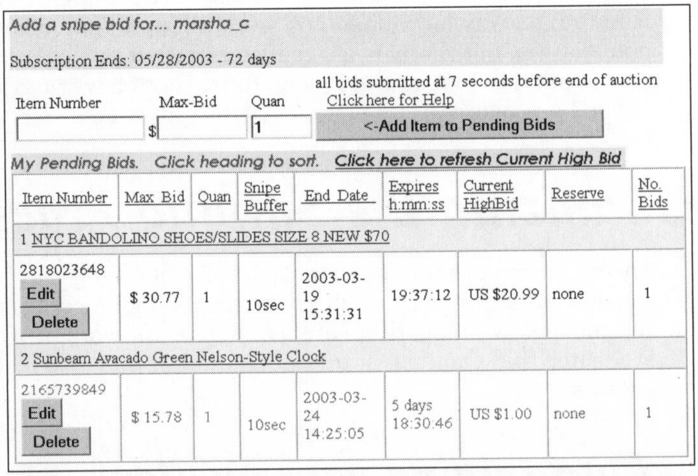

Add a snipe bid for... marsha_c

Subscription Ends: 05/28/2003 - 72 days

all bids submitted at 7 seconds before end of auction
Click here for Help

Item Number	Max-Bid	Quan	
	$	1	<-Add Item to Pending Bids

My Pending Bids. Click heading to sort. *Click here to refresh Current High Bid*

Item Number	Max Bid	Quan	Snipe Buffer	End Date	Expires h:mm:ss	Current HighBid	Reserve	No. Bids
1 NYC BANDOLINO SHOES/SLIDES SIZE 8 NEW $70								
2818023648 Edit Delete	$ 30.77	1	10sec	2003-03-19 15:31:31	19:37:12	US $20.99	none	1
2 Sunbeam Avacado Green Nelson-Style Clock								
2165739849 Edit Delete	$ 15.78	1	10sec	2003-03-24 14:25:05	5 days 18:30:46	US $1.00	none	1

Figure 3-3: Easily place snipes in advance by using the BidRobot Web site.

My Auctions: **Thursday, March 20, 2003 15:43:25 PST (eBay time)** ⬜ Maximize Size

If you have questions about the new site, read the Migration News page or contact the eSnipe Support Staff. Reminder that auction wins will require payment with BidPoints. **To Cancel or Edit a bid you entered on the new site, use the Info link on the right side of your My Auctions listing. Thank you!**

eSnipe Bid Wizard

Bid on this eBay auction Item: [   ]   [Next >>]

eSnipe Bid Wizard - eBay Bid Entry Results

eBay bid entry saved! Info link to review your bid entry. Your maximum bid amount is **$23.78** (eBay proxy bid). **eSnipe bid edit or cancel must be at least 5 minutes before bid time.** Email receipt was sent (Email settings).

| All | Archive | Bid Groups | Folders | Balance | Deleted | Old Site Bids |

Select	Item Description	Status	Item #	Bid Amount	Quantity	Buffer	Auction Bid Time	Info
☐	Shiseido Foundation Stick I2 Natural Lt Ivory	Ready to bid	2917446622	$23.78	1	6	03/20/2003 16:32:14	Info

Figure 3-4: A snipe ready to go at eSnipe.

Bidder's research software

Research software is the kind of software that is going to help you dig deep into a seller's feedback or check out a competitive bidder. Most software out there is for sellers, but you can find a couple of programs strictly for buyers. If you plan on spending any serious money at eBay, using a feedback evaluation software program might be worth the cost. Here is what's out there:

- ✓ **BayCheck Pro:** With this software, you can find out all about another eBay user. You can see his or her selling and bidding history, feedback received (isolating the neutrals and negatives to read without going through all the seller's e-mail) and the feedback the user has left for others. For a special free trial and a discount price of $14.99 for the software go to www. hammertap.com/coolebaytools/bargainhunter.html.

- ✓ **Safe2Bid:** This simple little program explores the feedback of any particular eBay user. It also separates the negatives and neutrals and works the percentages for you. More information is available at www.cricketsniper.com.

Knowing What You're Buying

Be sure that you know the actual street price of an item before you place a bid. The *street price* is the price that people actually pay — not the MSRP (manufacturer's suggested retail price).

You may be comfortable paying slightly more than the street price because eBay is so easy to use — after all, the item is delivered to your door, and you don't have to go to a bricks-and-mortar store to shop for the item. But it's good to know how much you can get the item for so you don't bid too much.

You can use the Internet to check prices for many items. In fact, several consumer Web sites are dedicated to serving savvy consumers by offering this information.

You can find computer item pricing at www.pricewatch.com. Prices for almost everything else can be found at a new site from Google, www.froogle.com.

Visit my Web site, www.coolebaytools.com, to use some Internet-wide search tools for all types of items on the Internet.

Chapter 4

Discovering Your My eBay Page

*O*ne of the super tools that eBay gives *all* its users is the My eBay page. I call it a page, but it's really an *area* — a group of several pages tagged together with tabs. The My eBay page gives you complete control of everything you are doing (or would like to do) at eBay. For example, sellers use this page to keep track of sales.

In this chapter, I show you how to take this tool and personalize it to keep all your eBay shopping organized — you can even make note of how much you spend (so you can stay within your shopping budget).

You can find a link to your My eBay pages immediately when you go to the eBay site. It is available from the top of the eBay Web page Navigation Bar, by clicking the link that points to My eBay.

If you haven't signed in, you can access your My eBay page by following these steps:

1. **On the top of any eBay page, click the My eBay link above the Navigation Bar.**

   You're sent to the My eBay sign in page.

2. **Type your User ID and password.**

   You can type in your registered e-mail address or your eBay User ID. Your User ID and e-mail address are interchangeable on the site.

3. **Alternatively, you can sign in with Microsoft Passport.**

   If you sign in with Passport, you go directly to your My eBay.

   If you ever forget your eBay password, go to `http://pages.ebay.com/services/registration/reqpass.html`. If you remember the answer to the question you were asked during the eBay registration process, you can create a new password immediately. (For registration information, see Chapter 1.)

4. **Click the Sign In button.**

   When you arrive at the target page (see Figure 4-1), you're presented with a page of links. You can choose

---

Welcome to eBay, queen-of-shopping

To change your sign in or display preferences, go to My eBay Preferences tab.

Where can we take you?
- Item I last looked at
- My eBay
- Sell your item
- Check out the Announcement Board for site updates

Figure 4-1: Signed in and ready to shop.

- **The My eBay Preferences tab:** In this area, you can customize how eBay will work for you based on your personal preferences. Keep reading this chapter for help on how to use this tool.

- **Item I Last Looked At:** If you were looking at an item at eBay, and realized you weren't signed, this link takes you back to that item.

- **My eBay:** Click this link to catch up on your eBay shopping. (See Figure 4-2.)

- **Sell Your Item:** Click this link when the time comes that you want to sell at eBay.

Figure 4-2: Your My eBay page is the hub for your eBay activities.

- **Announcement Board:** Click this link for site updates: This link brings you to the System Status Announcement page. This isn't a place that as a buyer you're going to visit often — it's where eBay reports current problems in the system.

5. **Click the My eBay link, and you're there!**

   From the My eBay page, you can click a tab to go to any of these places:

The My eBay page consists of seven tabs: Bidding/Watching, Selling, Favorites, Accounts, Feedback, Preferences, and All. Table 4-1 gives you the scoop about each of the tabs.

Table 4-1   What You Can Change on Your My eBay Page

Click Here	To See This on Your My eBay Page
Bidding/Watching	Every item for sale that you're watching, bidding on, and all items you've won and lost.
Selling	All the information about any items you're selling at eBay.
Favorites	A collection of links to your favorite categories, searches, and sellers and stores.

(continued)

Table 4-1 *(continued)*

Click Here	To See This on Your My eBay Page
Account	Your eBay account information, such as seller's fees and invoices.
Feedback	The most recent feedback comments about you and links that send you to all the feedback you've left and received. There's also a link to an area where you can respond to feedback.
Preferences	All the preferences that you can specify so that eBay performs just as you want it to.
All	All these options in one (very long) scrollable page.

You may change the order in which these items appear on the page by clicking the up or down arrows in the right-hand corner of the boxes. Click the up arrow once, and the selected box moves up one space on the page. Click the down arrow, and the box will move down one space.

Watching, Bidding, and Winning

The Bidding/Watching tab of the My eBay page helps you keep control of everything you're currently shopping for on the site. This is the page I check several times a day to see the progress of items I'm interested in.

This tab can be very handy because you can monitor the best deals and bargains that are closing within the next few hours. You can even set the downloadable eBay Toolbar so that an alarm goes off a few minutes before one of the auctions you're watching ends. See Chapter 3 for more on how to set-up this automated system.

Keeping track of items you've bid on

Every time you bid on an item at eBay, a record of your bidding action is posted in the Items I'm Bidding On area of your My eBay page (see Figure 4-3).

Items I'm Bidding On (4 Items)   ▶ See totals | All item details ⊕ ⊟

Items that you are currently winning are green and bold, those that you are **not** currently winning are red.

Item #	Start Price	Current Price	My Max Bid	Qty	# of Bids	Start Date	(PST) End Date	Time Left
LUX SATEEN COTTON*ItSCROLL*CAL KING SHEET SET								
2316647316	$47.97	$47.97	$47.97	1	1	Apr-08	Apr-18 23:56:01	0d 0h 3m
BEADED DIVA PURSE & LULU GUINNESS PARFUM								
2825081961	$39.99	$39.99	$39.99	1	1	Apr-17	Apr-20 06:25:05	1d 6h 32m
NYC ONEX WHITE SHOES/SANDALS SIZE 8 NEW $62								
2824596123	$19.49	$19.49	$19.49	1	1	Apr-14	Apr-21 14:19:23	2d 14h 27m
MARILYN MIGLIN PERFECT C SERUM NEW								
2923569484	$4.99	$6.01	$5.51	1	2	Apr-14	Apr-24 17:49:28	5d 17h 57m

Totals	Start Price	Current Price	My Max Bid	Total Qty	# of Bids
All items	$112.44	$113.46	$112.98	4	5
Items that I'm winning	$107.45	$107.45	$107.45	3	3

Figure 4-3: Items I'm bidding on.

In fact, the Items I'm Bidding On area displays a clickable link to the item; the amount of your maximum bid, the current price, the auction's end date (as well as a counter style Time Left column). If you are the leading bidder, your price appears in green, and if you're not, it appears in red. (If you're participating in a Dutch auction, your current bid isn't color coded.)

The dollar values for all your active bids are totaled automatically at the bottom of the Items I'm Bidding On area. This is an invaluable tool so that you can know just how much you're spending at one time or another.

Watching the progress of the auction from here can be very strategic. You can observe how much bidding action there is on an item before you decide to jump back in and bid again. If an item's price is getting too high for your liking, you might just want to search eBay for another one of the item so that you can get in on a bargain instead.

Counting the items you've won

After you win an item, the information you need automatically goes to the Items I've Won area of the My eBay page, shown in Figure 4-4. From here, you can pay for the item via PayPal (or see if your payment has already gone through) and go back to the auction

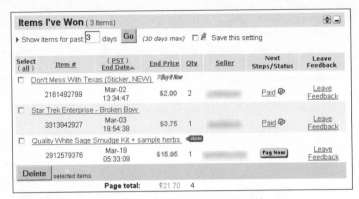

Figure 4-4: Counting my goodies in the Items I've Won area.

item page to print it out. You also can check out from here (if you haven't paid). But wait, there's more. There's also a link that allows you to leave feedback for the seller once you've received your item.

You can change the number of days you'd like to see reflected (up to 30 days) in the chart below. Notice that there is a box with a small push-pin icon with the words Save This Setting. Click in the box if you want the My eBay page to remember the number of days you've input that you want as your default. eBay's basic default for the display is two days.

Watching the items you want

Your Bidding/Watching page has an area where you can *watch* some items. From this area you can observe the bidding action on items that interest you without showing your hand to the competition — that you're interested in the item. You can see the number of bids that were placed on the item and see how fast the price is rising (or not).

You have a limited number of items that you can watch — just 30 and then eBay cuts you off. Silly eBay would rather have you *bid* on items rather than watch them!

When you've found an auction that you want to keep track of, look for the teeny pair of binoculars in the right column at the top of the auction. That's the Watch This Item link. Click the link, and the item listing becomes active in your Items I'm Watching area.

At the bottom of the My eBay page is a group of links that can take you to related areas at eBay. Before you freak out because you have a question about something at eBay, double-check the bottom of the page. These links link to eBay's basic help information.

Knowing the items you lost

The My eBay page has a section letting you know when you've been outbid and lost an item, as shown in Figure 4-5. This option isn't there just to rub your nose in all the auctions you've lost — it's actually a very handy tool that lets you search the seller's items for a similar item, or search the category for a similar item with a click of the mouse.

Items I Didn't Win (5 Items)						
▶ Show items for past 7 days **Go** (30 days max) ☐ Save this setting						
Select (all)	Item #	My Max Bid	End Price	# of Bids	View seller's other items	Find other items in this category
☐ NWT Sony PCGA-PRF1A Vaio Docking Station						
	3403016378	$60.00	$205.00	32	View seller's other items	Find now
☐ Minnetonka Women's Kilty Swede Mocs Size 8						
	2814028937	$10.00	$13.05	4	View seller's other items	Find now
☐ Minnetonka Moccasins white ladies sz 8 NEW						
	2814036581	$8.99	$12.50	3	View seller's other items	Find now
☐ GOLDEN BOYS BANDSTAND-FABIAN-Autograph-60's						
	2160804431	$37.01	$60.00	9	View seller's other items	Find now
☐ Raymor HOWARD MILLER Clock NELSON Eames						
	2510612172	$15.00	$255.00	17	View seller's other items	Find now
Delete selected items						
					< Previous Showing Items 1 - 5 of 5 Next >	

Figure 4-5: Items I *(sniff)* didn't win.

Keeping Track of Your Favorites

The best part of cruising eBay for bargains is finding items you never knew you wanted or needed. (I just saw a great deal on a 1950s candy dish — who'd have guessed that I needed it?) People have so many varied interests that the Favorites page is the perfect way to keep up with the many things you want to look for regularly.

You can list 4 of your favorite categories for browsing, 15 of your favorite searches and 15 of your favorite sellers (or eBay stores).

By listing your favorites, you can build your own personal eBay mall, populated with only the types of items you're interested in.

Setting up your favorite searches

There may be certain things that you are *always* looking for at eBay. Say you plan to search frequently for a Callaway Seven Heaven Wood — whatever — add it to your list of favorite searches (see Figure 4-6), and you won't have to retype *Callaway Seven Heaven Wood* more than once. (Now there's a blessing!) By organizing your favorite searches, you can search for your favorite items with a click of your mouse on the <u>Search Now</u> link.

Be sure to use all the search trick shortcuts I show you in the table in Chapter 10 because these searches are not performed in the search box. These are single-line searches that you normally would perform from the small search boxes on the eBay pages.

My eBay - Hello <u>marsha c (2073)</u> ★ me stores

<u>Bidding/Watching</u>   <u>Selling Manager</u>   **Favorites**   <u>Accounts</u>   <u>Feedback</u>   <u>Preferences</u>   <u>All</u>

Go to: <u>My Favorite Categories</u> | <u>My Favorite Searches</u> | <u>My Favorite Sellers/Stores</u>   ⑦ **Questions**

My Favorite Searches

▸<u>Add new Search</u> ▾ ▬

Select (all)	My Search criteria	Search for items	Email Me when new items appear
☐	broguiere's	<u>Search Now</u>	☐
☐	("fur real", furreal)	<u>Search Now</u>	☐
☐	(macys, macy's) parade	<u>Search Now</u>	☐
☐	(debox, deboxed, deboxer)	<u>Search Now</u>	☐
☐	"case of"	<u>Search Now</u>	☐
☐	rodrique	<u>Search Now</u>	☐
☐	onex	<u>Search Now</u>	☐
☐	ea@	<u>Search Now</u>	☐
☐	"ex wife" -vhs -cd -dvd -videos -book	<u>Search Now</u>	☐
☐	lulu gu* (purse, bag)	<u>Search Now</u>	☐

Figure 4-6: My favorite searches.

To set up a favorite search, follow these steps:

1. **Click the <u>Add New Search</u> link on the Favorites page.**

   The eBay Search page appears.

2. **Type your key search words and perform your search.**

3. **When the results come up, scroll to the bottom of the page and click the <u>Save This Search</u> link.**

You can select three of your favorite searches to be e-mailed to you daily (or whenever new items appear). For example, there are some lesser-known artists who I like; I've set up my favorite searches so that I'll get an e-mail message whenever one of the artist's items shows up for sale at eBay.

Choosing your favorite categories

The Favorite categories area has got to be eBay's cruel joke. For some reason, you're only allowed to select *four* categories on your Favorites page! Certainly that's not enough for an inveterate shopper! But four it is, and you must select your four. Click the link on the top-right of this box to change or set your categories through eBay's drop-down boxes.

To set up your favorite categories, follow these steps:

1. **Select the main category you're interested in.**

If the category is divided into subcategories, an arrow appears at the end of the category name.

2. **Click the subcategory you're interested in.**

If you see *another* arrow, yet *another* subcategory box opens.

3. **Click the subcategory that you like.**

And so on, until you reach a category that doesn't end in an arrow.

You must perform this clickfest four times so that you can select all four categories (see Figure 4-7).

If you want to link to fewer than four categories, just select as many as you want to monitor, then click Submit. Only the categories you selected are listed.

You can't choose a big category — you have to choose a subcategory.

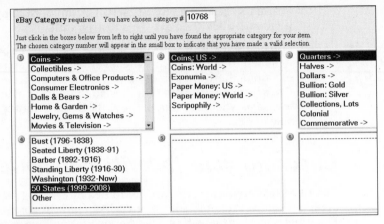

Figure 4-7: Selecting your favorite categories.

The items at eBay are all organized in a cornucopia of categories (see Chapter 2 for more information). If you click a category, you see a category number. If you know the number of your favorite category, you can just type it into the category number box when you set up your favorite categories, and not go through the drop-down menu selection process.

When you've gone through the process and selected your four categories, your favorite categories area will look like the one in Figure 4-8.

Figure 4-8: My favorite categories *(this week).*

To browse your favorite categories, you have to select one of the four links offered:

- ✔ **Current:** By clicking on this link you'll see every item currently being auctioned in the category, with the most recent listings shown first.

  With this search, you may end up with thousands of items to wade through.

- ✔ **New Today:** This option shows all items put up for sale within the prior 24 hours, with the newest listings shown first.

- ✔ **Ending Today:** Shows you every auction that is closing within the next 24 hours, in the order of ending time. The ending time is printed in red if the auction closes within five hours, and those ending first are shown first.

  A more efficient search, especially in a category with tens of thousands of items, would be in the New Today or Ending Today link. These links trim the number of listed items to a controllable number.

- ✔ **Going, Going, Gone:** Shows auctions in this category that are ending in the next five hours. This link offers a fun way to find items you can snipe. (See Chapter 3 for the lowdown on the fine art of getting bargains through sniping.)

Choosing your favorite sellers and stores

When you've been shopping eBay for awhile, you will find that certain sellers carry a type of merchandise that interests you. By saving their User IDs in this area, you'll be able to revisit their current auctions without having to run a seller search from the search area. (See Chapter 10 for more details on searches.)

The purpose of the My eBay page is to have all your controls in one area. Figure 4-9 shows a favorite sellers area.

You may add a new seller by clicking the <u>Add New Seller/Store</u> link in the upper-right corner of the box.

My Favorite Sellers/Stores			▸Add new ▲ ▢ Seller/Store
Select (all)	Seller	Store Name	View seller's other items
☐	aunt*patti (605) ☆ me ◄stores	Patti's Potpourri	Visit seller's eBay Store
☐	bargainland-liquidation (25399) ⚡ me ◄stores	Bargainland-Liquidation	Visit seller's eBay Store
☐	dmurphy4@yahoo.com (4818) ☆ ◄stores	GraMur Supply Co	Visit seller's eBay Store
☐	marsha_c (2074) ☆ me ◄stores	Marsha Collier's Fabulous Finds	Visit seller's eBay Store
☐	mrswarren (1221) ☆ me ◄stores	Pretty Girlie Things	Visit seller's eBay Store
☐	rejinsf (40) ☆		View seller's other items
Delete	selected sellers/stores		

Figure 4-9: Your My eBay Favorite Sellers area.

Feedback Central

In Chapter 5, I talk all about the importance of feedback to the eBay community. In the Feedback area of the My eBay page (see Figure 4-10), you can keep track of all your feedback duties.

When you click the Feedback tab, you can see your current eBay User ID card on the right, and on the left is an area that directs you on how to leave feedback to other eBay members.

Figure 4-10: The Feedback tab on the My eBay page.

The Leaving Feedback Links area gives you an all-in-one place to a link to all feedback duties. Here you can find places to

- ✔ Find all item listings from the last 90 days that you haven't left feedback for. (For shame!)

- ✔ Review and respond to feedback left for you. Responding to feedback is especially important, especially if the feedback is less than stellar. (Every story has two sides.)

- ✔ See all Feedback you have left for others. If you want to re-examine feedback that you've left, this is the place.

Below these boxes is a listing of all your feedback dating back to your first transaction at eBay.

Setting Your eBay Preferences

Visit the Preferences tab to change the way eBay reacts to your sign in information. You can set eBay to require your password every time you bid or perform eBay tasks or not. It's up to you. You can also set up your viewing preferences, like how many items come up on one page when you perform a search.

But the most important part of this area is the important links at the bottom of the page. These links lead you to locations where you can change your e-mail address (without losing your feedback), change your User ID, or change your password. There's also a link to change your home address on record.

Keeping all your contact information up-to-date at eBay is very important. If eBay ever finds that any of the contact information is wrong, you may have your membership suspended.

You also see a link that allows you to input your text messaging number for your mobile phone. That way, eBay can notify you on your mobile phone when you get outbid in an auction and when you win an item (if your mobile service offers this option, of course). (Select these options by clicking the <u>Change My Notification Preferences</u> link.)

Part II
Staying Safe While Shopping at eBay

The 5th Wave — By Rich Tennant

"Well no, it's not that comfortable, but the opening bid was only 3 dollars. Who would pass that up?"

In this part. . .

Part II covers the ways to stay safe while shopping at eBay (and the Internet in general). You want to get the bargains — not become a victim. The information here can keep you safe and smart. Remember, the dangers only occur when we try to take shortcuts — always do your due diligence before handing out your hard-earned money.

Chapter 5

Feedback: The Heart of Safe Trading

- -

In This Chapter

▶ Understanding feedback basics

▶ Scrutinizing a seller's reputation

▶ Doling out feedback responsibly

- -

*O*ne of eBay's strong suits has been the formation of a sense of community through its use of message boards, topical chats, and feedback. Many experts say the reason that eBay has succeeded where dozens of other dot com auction sites have failed is that eBay has always paid close attention to the needs of its users.

In its first few months of existence, the fledgling eBay (then called Auction Web) was marred with a few simple misunderstandings between some buyers and sellers. If an item arrived damaged or a little too late, for example, buyers would jump to conclusions and complain to eBay about sellers. And sellers had plenty of complaints, as well, especially about payments.

It soon became clear to eBay's three employees that they did not have time to adjudicate member disputes. And thus, the feedback system was born. I discuss the feedback system in this chapter.

Self-Policing: The eBay Way

Even in the early days, the concept was clear. Pierre and his employees figured that if users complained openly (for all other members to see), feedback would be more genuine — not so much *flaming* as *constructive*. The "do unto others" philosophy prevailed, and above all else, Pierre tried to encourage buyers and sellers to give each other the benefit of the doubt and to conduct themselves professionally. But the *piece de resistance* of the feedback policy, the part that really makes eBay work, is the fact that Pierre and his staff encouraged users to give positive feedback as often as they give negative or neutral feedback.

The benefits of the feedback policy are immediately clear. Before even placing a bid, a buyer (that's you) can check on the experience other eBay buyers have had doing business with this seller. For example, you can see whether

- ✔ Items in a seller's previous auctions shipped quickly.
- ✔ Items were packed carefully.
- ✔ Communication was clear and frequent.

You can have more information about an eBay seller in two minutes than you have when you walk into a new store in your own neighborhood.

Every eBay member has a feedback rating. Buyers rate sellers; sellers rate buyers — no one is immune. A seller might comment on how quickly you pay for an item, and how well you communicated or how you reacted to a problem.

Introducing your feedback rating

After every member's User ID there is a number. This number is a *net figure* of the positive comments that were left for that eBay user. What that means is if you get 50 positive comments and 49 negative comments, your feedback rating is 1.

For every positive comment you receive, you get a plus one (+1). For every negative comment, you get a minus one (-1). Theoretically, if you play nice, your feedback rating grows as you spend more time buying (and selling) at eBay.

The number, as it grows, shows not only how good a customer (and seller, if you go that route) you are, but also how experienced you are at doing business on the site. If your rating sinks to negative four (-4), you're suspended from using the eBay system. Forever.

You may also get a neutral comment. A neutral comment is neither negative nor positive and doesn't change the number that appears after your User ID. Neutral comments are used most often when someone is not completely happy with a transaction, but not so unhappy that he or she chooses to destroy someone else's reputation over the situation.

Getting your star

When you first join eBay, it seems like everyone at eBay has a star except for you. It's so unfair isn't it? Well, not really. The stars of many colors are awarded based on the amount of positive feedback that you have. When you receive a feedback rating of 10, you will get a gold star (just like in school).

You may notice stars of other colors — even shooting stars; Table 5-1 gives you the lowdown on what each star color represents.

Table 5-1 Star Colors and Your Feedback Rating	
Star Color	*Feedback Rating*
Gold star	10 to 49
Blue star	50 to 99
Turquoise star	100 to 499
Purple	500 to 999
Red star	1,000 to 4,999
Green star	5,000 to 9,999
Gold shooting star	10,000 to 24,999
Turquoise shooting star	25,000 to 49,999
Purple shooting star	50,000 to 99,999
Red shooting star	100,000 and higher

When you reach a higher level, I assure you that you will get a silly tingly feeling of accomplishment. It's all part of being a member of the eBay community.

Scrutinizing a Seller's Reputation

You've finally found an item you'd like to buy. Don't place that bid just yet! Studying the seller's feedback will supply you with a good deal of information about the reputation of your potential trading partner.

The more expensive your transaction, the more intense your investigation may need to be. An unblemished feedback rating may not be as significant on a $9 purchase as it is for a $200 purchase.

I want you to be thoroughly educated in how the feedback system works. I'm not trying to be bossy. I'm just saying that buyers and sellers (especially those of us who have been using eBay for several years) take this stuff very seriously.

Still, if you're just a dabbler, I can understand why you might want to learn the light version of the eBay feedback system and save the high-octane rendition of a feedback investigation for when you decide to buy a yacht, or the British Crown Jewels.

Conducting light seller scrutiny

As you look at the items for sale at eBay (both in auctions and in fixed-price sales), you'll notice that along with every auction listing you can find information about the seller. This is eBay's Seller Information box. (Figure 5-1 shows you a composite of three unique Seller Information boxes.)

Figure 5-1: Seller Information boxes from three different sellers, including me.

Consider a quick glance at the Seller Information box to be the light version of a feedback investigation. If your potential purchase is for an item that's worth a few dollars to you, and the Seller Information box shows a 99-100 percent positive feedback percentage, as in the first example in Figure 5-1, you're probably safe.

However, if the Seller Information box looks closer to the second example, and you're looking at a pricier item, it's time for a more thorough analysis.

The Seller Information box gives you a condensed version of the seller's feedback reputation. It always includes the seller's User ID and feedback rating, including his or her star award level. But the Seller Information box also contains some other important information, including the following:

- ✔ Whether the seller is a Power Seller (I discuss Power Selling in Chapter 6).

- ✔ Whether the seller has an About Me page (see more about the About Me page later in this chapter).

- ✔ Whether the seller has an eBay Store (see Chapter 16 for details). If so, a small price tag appears.

- ✔ A pair of sunglasses (known as *shades* in the eBay vernacular) to show if the user is new or has changed his or her User ID in the past 30 days.

- ✔ The seller's *positive feedback percentage*. This percentage is calculated by dividing the total of the seller's *unique* positive feedback comments by the total of the unique positive and negative feedback comments (see "Getting a comprehensive sense of a seller's feedback" for more on how eBay defines *unique* positive feedback comments).

- ✔ How long the seller has been a member of the eBay community.

- ✔ The seller's home country.

- ✔ Links to read the seller's feedback reviews, to view his or her other auctions (see Chapter 3 for why this is an important link), ask the seller a question (see Chapter 2), and a Safe Trading Tips link.

Even though the seller in the second example has an overall higher feedback rating, the percentage of positive comments is a little lower, and suggests further examination.

Checking the seller's About Me page

If you notice that Joe Seller has a small Me icon next to his or her User ID, click the icon to learn more about him.

Every eBay member may have his or her own home page at eBay called the About Me page (you can have one, too). The About Me page is where members talk about themselves, their businesses, and their collections. (You can find my About Me page at: `http:// members.ebay.com/aboutme/marsha_c`).

I came across the About Me page shown in Figure 5-2 when I was looking at an auction for a Limoge plate. This page is a great example of how eBay members show their personalities and build trustworthy person-to-person (rather than computer-to-computer) relationships with other members of the eBay community.

If a new seller (without a lot of feedback) smartly puts up an About Me page and talks about his or her eBay goals and business, you may feel more comfortable about doing business with the seller.

Hello! Thanks for checking out...

specializing in new and gently-used quality children's clothing

Welcome! My name is Christine, and I'm mom to 3 great kids. I have a full-time job and ventured into selling on eBay part-time, where I specialize in quality, name-brand children's clothing, from gently-used to Brand New! I have to admit...I'm quite the "shop-a-holic", and having a 3-year-old little girl only justifies my condition! My older two are out of the stage where *I* can still dress them, so I'm having a blast with my youngest! I have so many clothes, it's like having my own little boutique! I have also come to admire the talent and uniqueness of the many great children's clothing designers right here on eBay!

My number one priority is making sure each transaction goes smoothly. If there are ever any questions or concerns, please e-mail me and I'll be happy to work with you. *I'll also have other great items to offer, so please check back often!*

Thanks for visiting!

Figure 5-2: An example About Me page.

Getting a comprehensive sense of a seller's feedback

When you consider buying a more expensive item, be sure to click the seller's feedback number when you visit the auction item page. Clicking on the number shows you the member's feedback summary and ID card, shown in Figure 5-3.

After you click the feedback number, there are several things you should examine if you're a savvy, security-minded shopper.

Feedback Summary	ebY ID card		marsha_c (2036) ★ ⚡Power Seller me stores	
2359 positives. **2037** are from unique users.	Member since: Sunday, Jan 05, 1997 Location: United States			
	Summary of Most Recent Reviews			
		Past 7 days	Past month	Past 6 mo.
	Positive	7	52	566
17 neutrals. **14** were converted from users no longer registered .	Neutral	0	0	1
	Negative	0	0	0
	Total	7	52	567
	Bid Retractions	0	0	0
0 negatives. **0** are from unique users.	View marsha_c 's eBay Store	Auctions	ID History	Feedback About Others		

Figure 5-3: Member feedback summary and ID card.

Feedback summary

On the left side of the page you see the feedback summary and on the right, the seller's ID card. Here there are significant things to note:

> ✔ **Positive feedback comments:** You may notice that the actual number of positive comments is higher then the net positive figure. This is because every eBay community member can comment about another member as often as he or she wants, but the comment only counts once in the feedback rating. The rating is called a *net rating* because it's based on comments from *unique* users.
>
> For example, if you buy an item from me, and we leave each other feedback (glowingly positive, I'm sure), and then next month I buy something from you, the feedback we leave on

the second transaction (again, glowingly positive) doesn't count toward our total feedback rating. However, the feedback does appear on the feedback summary page. You can only affect each other's feedback rating by 1.

✔ **Neutral comments:** Neutral comments are usually left when a party wasn't thrilled with the transaction, but nothing happened that was really bad enough to leave a dreaded, reputation-ruining negative comment. You may also notice that some long-time eBay users have neutral comments that were converted from users no longer registered.

For a very short while eBay had a policy that when a member was suspended (yes, members do get suspended) or the member chose to cancel his or her eBay membership, eBay turned all the feedback it member ever left or received (whether it was positive or negative) into neutral feedback.

This policy didn't last for very long because the eBay members put up such a fuss that the eBay Powers That Be listened and stopped the practice. Unfortunately, eBay didn't rescind the neutrals that had been put into place.

✔ **Negative comments:** The number of negative comments may also vary, just like the positives, because only one comment is allowed per "unique user." (Information on when to leave what kind of feedback appears later in this chapter.)

Member ID card

On the right side of this comprehensive feedback is the eBay Member ID card, which carries historic information about the member:

✔ **Identification information:** Click the User ID to see an e-mail form so that you can send an e-mail to the member through eBay's e-mail system.

✔ **Summary of most recent reviews:** In a snapshot, you can see the seller's recent eBay history for the past week, month, and six-month period. This data is very useful because often the last couple of month's transactions tell the tale. If a previously reliable eBay seller has decided to join the Dark Side, this is where the evidence shows up first. New negative comments from different buyers are signs of danger, even if the seller has an overall high rating.

If the last few transactions are negative in the recent reviews, think twice about doing business with the seller, but that doesn't mean that you should count the seller out completely. If the item is *really* a must-have, click the ID of the person (or persons) who left the negative feedback, and ask politely for details so that you can make your own decisions. Sadly, many buyers leave negative feedback for a seller before giving the seller an opportunity to make things right, so by getting the details you can make your own decisions.

✔ **Bid retractions:** A history of bidding on items and then changing one's mind is a signal more for a seller to note than a buyer. As a buyer, you may, under certain circumstances, retract your bid (see Chapter 2). Each time you retract your bid from an auction, the retraction shows up in this area. Sellers often check this area to determine a bidder's reliability.

✔ **Member links:** In this location, you can find links that can give you more information about the member, such as links to the member's eBay Store, (if the seller has one, of course), his or her other auctions (where you can see if the seller is experienced in selling the type of item you are looking to buy), his or her ID history (where you can view the seller's past User IDs, if any) and feedback the seller may have left about others.

Checking the type of feedback someone leaves about others can give you a real insight into his or her personality. When considering making a big purchase, I always check this area; it really helps me know the type of person I'm dealing with.

When you read feedback that makes nasty slams at the other person, or if the person uses rude words or phrases when leaving feedback, you may be dealing with a loose cannon.

Reading feedback reviews

Scrolling down the feedback history page, you'll be able to read the actual reviews left by other eBay members. In Figure 5-4, you'll see a sample of my current feedback. You see each the member's User ID, along with his or her feedback and comment.

Feedback Reviews for marsha_c		Feedback Help | FAQ

Feedback Reviews for marsha_c Feedback Help | FAQ

leave feedback for marsha_c   If you are marsha_c : Respond to comments   marsha_c was the **Seller = S** marsha_c was the **Buyer = B**

Left by	Date	Item#	S/B
____ (402) ☆ m⊜	Mar-07-03 13:34:34 PST	2914770525	S

Praise : Buy Marsha's books. Excellent teacher. I have profited greatly. A+++++++++

| ____ (32) ☆ | Mar-07-03 07:09:03 PST | 3003142415 | S |

Praise : fast and efficient! AAA+++++

| ____ (26) ☆ | Mar-07-03 05:17:38 PST | 2912834046 | S |

Praise : Rcvd your book...THANKS......It is Wonderful...A++++++++++++++

| ____ (26) ☆ | Mar-06-03 21:58:21 PST | 3001532916 | S |

Praise : Very satisfied, loved the merchandise, fast and very good at keeping in touch

| ____ (1196) ★ | Mar-06-03 19:05:12 PST | 3010607432 | B |

Praise : Super transaction,Recommend this eBayer highly,Thanks!!!!!!!!!!!!!!!!!

| ____ (151) ☆ | Mar-05-03 07:00:51 PST | 3001317054 | S |

Praise : Excellent Transaction, Quick shipping, AAAA++++

Figure 5-4: Feedback review page.

Here's what else you see:

- ✔ The date the feedback was left, along with a clickable link to the transaction. You can click the link to the item, as long as it was for a relatively recent transaction (items generally remain in the eBay database for about 90 days).

- ✔ Either see an S or a B on the far right side of each comment. S stands for the seller in the transaction, and B stands for the buyer.

  Many independent eBay sellers are experienced buyers as well as sellers — they have an excellent grasp of how eBay feels from a customer's point of view and expertly know how to handle any of your concerns.

Here are some tips for assessing feedback, depending on the situation:

- ✔ When buying from a seller that sells the same item repetitively, use the clickable links to the past transactions to check if *other* buyers were pleased with their purchases.

- ✔ When you come across neutral or negative feedback, as shown in Figure 5-5, look for the seller's response. A seller or a buyer may respond to the feedback by clicking the <u>Respond to Comments</u> link (refer to Figure 5-4).

The feedback system relies on the expectation that members give each other the benefit of the doubt. When you come across negative (or neutral) feedback about a seller, look for the seller's response and see whether the problem was resolved before making your final judgment. You may even see a *follow-up* feedback comment from the buyer saying that everything has been settled.

At eBay, feedback cannot be removed, unless both parties go through mediation (see Chapter 6).

		Mar-13-02 21:09:40 PST	1314342865	S

(1796) ★ me

Neutral : Product was of poor quality and overpriced. Bad buy on my part.
Response by marsha_c - Wish customer had emailed me, would have refunded money.
Retail $150 paid $87.

Figure 5-5: A seller's response to feedback.

Leaving Responsible Feedback

Almost any eBay seller will tell you that one of his or her pet peeves about the eBay feedback system is that new community members tend to leave neutral, or, even worse, *negative* feedback the moment a shipment arrives and something is wrong.

Here's what you need to know to avoid getting a bad rap for being too hard on sellers.

Missing or damaged shipments

When the package leaves the seller's hands, it is *literally* (and completely) out of his hands. If UPS, Federal Express Ground, or Federal Express Air ships your package, the tracking number can track the item. Tracking offered by the U.S. Post Office can be casual (at best), and is often not scanned until the package is delivered to your door, thus negating the trackability (for lack of a better term) of the package. Here are a few things to remember:

✔ **Be sure you know when the seller plans to ship the merchandise, so there is less question about when it will probably arrive.** If this information isn't stated in the auction description, use the <u>Ask the Seller a Question</u> link to find out *before* you buy to see if the shipping schedule matches your needs.

 ✓ **If you do not pay the seller extra money to purchase insurance before your item is shipped, it is unfair to hold the seller responsible for damaged or lost shipments.** Period. End of story.

 ✓ **Open your packages immediately upon receipt.** A seller can't make a claim on an item that you report damaged in shipping a month after it arrives, so leaving negative feedback at that point is unfair. Most shippers insist that any and all damage must be reported within five days of receipt. Also, if damage has occurred, keep all packing materials for inspection by the carrier. If you fail to save these materials, the carrier may not accept your claim, and you will have no further recourse.

 ✓ **There is not much that a seller can do about a missing package.** Sellers can't even make a claim on a postal shipment until 30 days have passed since mailing.

 ✓ **If the item never arrives, only the sender can file a claim with the shipping company and must produce all shipping receipts.** It's only fair to notify the seller immediately upon receiving a damaged shipment, either by e-mail or telephone. Leaving negative feedback before contacting the seller to help you make the claim is just plain unjust.

You shouldn't notify the seller of conditions using feedback. Use e-mail.

USPS information you can use

To file a claim with the U.S. Postal Service, visit the USPS Web site (`http://pe.usps.gov/text/dmm/s010.htm#Rgf16915`).

Only the sender can file a claim for the complete loss of a registered, insured, COD, or Express Mail item (including merchandise return service parcels to which special.

Either the sender of the recipient can file a claim for damage or if some or all of the contents of an article are missing.

Item doesn't meet your expectations

If the item arrives and it isn't as described in the item description, e-mail the seller. Communication is a good thing. Give the seller the opportunity to work things out with you.

Most sellers feel that customers are important *(essential!)* to their eBay business and want to preserve their reputation. If you don't give a seller a chance, he or she can't make things right. Keep in mind these facts:

- ✔ If an item arrives damaged and is brand new and sent in the manufacturer's sealed box, the damage could have happened at the manufacturer, and the seller might never have known about it.

- ✔ A seller may not be as experienced in a particular area of collecting as you are. If you didn't ask all the necessary questions before bidding, you may have just gotten what the seller assumed was a collectible. It's up to the buyer to ask questions before placing a bid at eBay — which is a legally binding contract to purchase.

- ✔ Don't jump to leave negative feedback if you receive the wrong item. The seller might have mixed up the labels during shipping. Just notify the seller. He or she will no doubt work out the mistake with you.

Most importantly, the seller should be given the chance to prove he or she cares. If you can't come to terms with the seller, try contacting SquareTrade (see Chapter 6) for online dispute resolution. If you feel you're a victim of fraud, you can apply for eBay's fraud insurance (see Chapter 7).

Leaving Feedback

Remember that feedback cannot be retracted. You are responsible for your words. They will remain on the eBay site forever with your User ID next to them for all to see. Be sure to leave a simple, factual, and *unemotional* statement.

Important things to mention in your feedback are

- ✔ How satisfied you were with your purchase
- ✔ The quality of the packaging
- ✔ The promptness of shipping
- ✔ The seller's professionalism
- ✔ The level of communication

If you must leave a negative feedback comment, know that you will probably get one in return because if you couldn't resolve things without a problem, chances are the seller wasn't very happy with the trading experience either. Try to work things out first!

Chapter 6

Shopping Safely

In This Chapter
▶ Using ID Verify
▶ Making a SquareTrade
▶ Shopping internationally
▶ Using Transrow for bid verification

I am a big proponent of taking responsibility for my own actions. When I mess up, I admit it (only to myself, of course, and then I immediately destroy all evidence of the debacle) and try not to make that same mistake again.

Maybe one reason I like eBay so much is because its sense of community revolves around the concept of personal responsibility (check out Chapter 5 for more information). So, what I'm about to tell you shouldn't be too surprising: You are responsible for your actions when you shop online. Be careful. Remember all the caveats I mention in this book. The feedback information in Chapter 5 is important, but not more so than the information I give you in this chapter.

As in life, if a deal at eBay looks too good to be true, it very well may be!

In this chapter, I show you a few solid things to consider in your eBay dealings.

First Warnings That Something's Not Right

Although feedback is your number one tool for assessing the legitimacy of a seller before you place a bid, the following information is essential for your protection, as well. Think twice if you see these items when you're shopping:

✔ **Pre-sale listings:** eBay permits sellers to list items for sale that are not currently in their possession, provided that the seller guarantees that the item can be shipped within 30 days from the end of the listing. However, the seller must state that the item is a pre-sale.

Unless you really, really need the item, or the seller has really outstanding feedback, 30 days is a long time to be without your money or an item — and it is no guarantee that the item will ever arrive. Before you bid, click the <u>Ask the Seller a Question</u> link to get a firm shipping date from the seller. If you can't get a hold of the seller, take it as a sign to move on. By the way, if you intend to pay for a pre-sale item using PayPal, take note — allows sellers only 20 days advance payment.

✔ **An impossible-to-find item:** Double-check a seller's feedback, if he or she is selling large quantities of hard-to-find items, especially during the holidays when the hot ticket is an item that's selling for double or triple the suggested retail price. People tend to throw caution to the wind when they see an item they want desperately that's sold out everywhere else in the known universe. Read the seller's feedback to see if people who have ordered this item in recent auctions have actually received the item.

✔ **Professional photos:** Is the seller using the same photos in multiple auctions? Does the photo look like it has been taken from the manufacturer's Web site? A computer-savvy person can easily take a picture from the manufacturer and claim it as his or her own. The more a photograph looks as if it was taken by the seller, the better the chance that the seller actually has the item.

✔ **E-mail solicitations:** You may receive solicitations from sellers offering to sell you an item you recently bid on for a lower price. Although the seller may be earnest, you will not be protected by eBay in any transaction that doesn't happen on the eBay site. In other words, just because you're doing business with an eBay member doesn't mean you're doing a transaction at eBay. The fact is that hucksters will do anything they can to get around eBay's policies.

Using ID Verify

ID Verify is a tool that is available to both buyers and sellers. Members who are new to the site, and members who choose not to provide credit card information when registering to become eBay sellers, tend to use it most frequently.

The ID Verify icon (shown in Figure 6-1) appears next to an eBay member's User ID if he or she has applied for, and passed the verification process.

The process is simple, and it allows new users of eBay to show other members that they are earnest in their desire to become a responsible member of the community. It means that your identification has been verified by the trusted organization, VeriSign.

Figure 6-1: The ID Verify icon.

If you're thinking about bidding in a new seller's auction (one that has little or low feedback — but, so far, all positive), the ID Verify icon shows that the seller has put some serious effort into establishing credibility. At least you know right off the bat that members who use ID Verify are who they say they are.

You might also like to use ID Verify, as well. There are benefits for buyers as well. Again, if you didn't provide a credit card number when you became a registered eBay member, ID Verify allows you to

✔ Bid on items at Sothebys.com through the eBay site

✔ Bid above $15,000 (lucky you!)

✔ Access the Mature Audiences Category

If you want these benefits, the cost is $5, and you'll be asked personal information such as your name, date of birth, social security number or driver's license number, and to identify credit card account information. Your ID Verify icon is valid until your home address or phone number changes. You submit all information using an encrypted, secure connection.

Introducing SquareTrade

Many sellers who are serious about their eBay business apply for a SquareTrade seal. SquareTrade was founded in 1999 to provide a way for online traders to ensure safer online transactions. To date, SquareTrade has resolved over 100,000 disputes, totaling $50 million in transactions. SquareTrade provides several services to the eBay community.

The SquareTrade seal program

Sellers who meet SquareTrade's stringent standards may subscribe to the SquareTrade seal (see Figure 6-2) and display it (proudly) in their auctions. A SquareTrade-reviewed seller meets the following criteria:

- **Identity verification:** SquareTrade has verified the seller's identity, contact information, or both the identity *and* the contact information.

- **Mediation commitment:** Should the need arise, the seal certifies that the seller agrees to enter mediation to resolve transaction-related issues, as well as to abide by any agreements that are the result of mediation processes.

- **Fraud protection:** By displaying the seal, the seller may be demonstrating that an additional layer of fraud protection (above and beyond that offered by eBay) is available for purchases. The additional fraud protection goes $200 over that offered by eBay's policy.

- **Selling standards:** To be sealed SquareTrade members, sellers must explicitly define their selling policies and maintain high customer service standards.

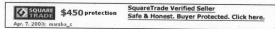

Figure 6-2: The SquareTrade seal is updated daily with a check on the seller's reputation.

Online dispute resolution

If you have a problem in a transaction, you may file your case with SquareTrade. SquareTrade will contact the other party, and the two of you may attempt to work things out through SquareTrade's automated, Web-based direct negotiation tool. The negotiation is done through a secure page and often works things out to both parties' satisfaction. There is no extra charge for this service for the SquareTrade member, and no charge at all for the other party.

If things don't work out, the next step is to involve an online mediator. The mediator works as a facilitator to produce solution-oriented discussion between the parties. Online mediators aren't judges or arbitrators, and will only recommend a resolution if the parties request it.

The party who files the case pays $20 for the mediator. This type of mediation costs a good deal more, but eBay subsidizes the majority of the costs involved.

If you ever get negative feedback (arghhh!) and both you and the other party come to terms to resolve the issue after the feedback is left, there is only one way that you can get that feedback removed. If you apply for SquareTrade mediation and the opposing party tells the mediator that he or she has agreed to its removal, the offending feedback will be expunged from your soon-to-be unblemished record.

Buying Internationally

Please be careful when doing business overseas. Especially watch out for counterfeit brand-name items. Even if you're in the right, if you've paid for an item, getting a refund may be impossible.

Bidding verification

If you decide to shoot the works and get involved in one of eBay's high-dollar (or high-profile) auctions, you will become familiar with a service called Transrow, an eBay preferred provider.

Transrow is a service that protects the seller from those who enjoy making spurious bids on items for fun. Before bidding on a very expensive item, you may see a link that says you must call the Transrow 1-800 number to prequalify, to be sure that your bid is in earnest. Once on the phone, Transrow verifies that you are who you say you are, and how you intend to pay for the item.

To see more information on Transrow (and to see a list of the auctions the business is currently working with at eBay), go to www.transrow.com.

Sometimes the risk of shopping with an overseas seller is necessary. I have done it, and many buyers at eBay do it all the time. Keep in mind a couple of tips to avoid getting duped in your international transactions:

- ✔ International shipping costs will be considerably higher.
- ✔ You may be on the hook for customs fees when the item arrives in your home country.
- ✔ For safety's sake, pay only through a third-party service like PayPal. Sending a money order to a foreign country is like mailing away cash.

PayPal will only send your payment to certain countries. The service keeps track of which countries are ravaged by fraud, and flatly refuses to do business where the risk is too great. PayPal maintains a page of countries that it does business with. When you check this page, be sure to read it closely.

In some cases, PayPal won't send your money to certain countries, but will let users send money to sellers. For a current list of the countries that PayPal *will* transact business in, go to http://www.paypal.com/cgi-bin/webscr?cmd=p/gen/approved_countries-outside.

Chapter 7

Protecting Yourself from Having a Bad Transaction

*I*n Chapter 6, I talked about things you can do to protect yourself when shopping at eBay.

You mustn't forget that eBay is a *venue*. When you bid, win, and pay for an item, you're doing business with *another person* using the eBay site. Technically, eBay's only function is that it created the online environment in which you and the seller could meet, shake hands, and do business. In other words, eBay has nothing to do with your transactions. That said, of course, eBay has a vested interest in making sure that your transactions go well, so that you'll come back and buy and sell more stuff. So eBay put policies into place for everyone's protection.

In this chapter, I go over what eBay has to offer in the way of protection.

Identifying What Makes a Transaction Fraudulent

At the outset, I'd like to get one thing straight: It's about *fraud*. What is fraud? Is it fraud when you get an item that isn't what you "thought" it would look like? Is it fraud when your item doesn't arrive and you neglected to pay additional for shipping insurance?

Is it fraud when you buy a diamond ring and a stunning cubic zirconium model arrives? Well, no, absolutely no — and yes.

According to the National Consumers League (www.fraud.org), online auctions top the online fraud list for 2002. Well, maybe. I think that if all the people who screamed "Fraud!" when their item arrived in *cerise cherry* instead of *raging red* were weeded out of the statistic, the online auction venue might have been lower on the list.

The fine line between *caveat emptor* (buyer beware) and fraud has to do with the questions you choose to ask. It is *your* responsibility to ask all possible questions before you buy; the seller doesn't have to tell you anything. That said, of course, the seller isn't allowed to lie to you.

Say you bid on a piece of bone china and when you pull the item out of the box you realize that it has a chip in it. Before you bid, did you ask whether there were any chips? If not, then you really weren't defrauded.

Well, okay. But it's not even *that* simple. You *may have been* defrauded if you didn't ask the seller about the condition because the seller listed the item as chip free or even as being in mint condition. Notice, I said may have been.

If the seller did advertise the bone china as mint, flawless, free of chips, or something like that, be sure to e-mail the seller and see if he or she was even aware of the flaw before you yell fraud. Maybe you can get your money back.

Communication and cooperation are central to being a successful eBay member. If you have a difference of opinion with another user, write a polite e-mail outlining your issues and offer to settle any dispute by phone. See Chapter 5 for tips on communicating after the auction ends and solving disputes *before* they turn aggressive, belligerent, or offensive. And don't forget to write fair, unemotional feedback about your transaction experiences.

Fraud Protection Program

Most transactions go off without a hitch. Sometimes, things go wrong. But of all the bad things that can happen (packages getting lost in the mail, items arriving that don't match the item description, and so on) less than 1/100th of 1 percent of eBay transactions turn out to be fraudulent. Even so, eBay has gone the distance by providing an insurance policy of sorts for eBay shoppers.

Even though I am very careful about who I am willing to do business with in the first place, I'm *also* always careful that my transactions are covered by eBay insurance. The way I figure it, the more business you do, the more likely that you'll eventually need insurance. That's just the way the law of averages works.

There are several types of insurance available to eBay buyers, as shown in Table 7-1.

Table 7-1	eBay Shopper's Insurance	
Type of Insurance	*Who Pays*	*Explanation*
Shipping insurance	Buyer	As the buyer, you must pay the seller the additional charge for package insurance. This will cover your purchase up to the insured amount while in transit through the U.S. Postal Service, UPS, or Federal Express.
eBay fraud protection	No charge	Buyer is automatically covered up to $200 when a purchase is made at eBay from an eBay seller.
PayPal insurance	No charge	If eBay agrees that you've been defrauded, and you've paid for your purchase through PayPal to a PayPal-verified seller (see Chapter 8) you're covered for an additional $200.
SquareTrade buyer protection program	No charge	SquareTrade will pay up to $500 (above and beyond any other insurance coverage you may have) if you have been defrauded by a SquareTrade seal member.

Getting eBay fraud insurance

The Fraud Protection Program provided by eBay covers the cost of purchase for an item that never makes it to your door. This coverage is only doled out if the package doesn't arrive because of a fraudulent transaction — it doesn't cover shipping errors or other mishaps.

You're also covered if you get the item and you find it to be materially different from the item in the auction's description. (Remember the definition of fraud? If not, see "Identifying What Makes a Transaction Fraudulent" earlier in this chapter.)

eBay insurance covers you to a maximum of $200 coverage per transaction; minus a $25 deductible. So if you file a $50 claim, you get $25. If you file a $5,000 claim, you get only $175. (But I hope that if you're going to spend that kind of scratch at eBay, you protect yourself by dealing with a PayPal- or SquareTrade-verified seller.)

To file a claim, you must file a Fraud Alert at eBay's Fraud Reporting System within 30 (and no later than 60) days after the auction ends. I doubt you'll ever need the link, but if you ever need to file a Fraud Alert, go to `http://crs.ebay.com/aw-cgi/ebayisapi.dll?crsstartpage`.

After you file the alert, eBay e-mails you a link to the final online protection claim form. You fill it out, return it to eBay, and you should have results in a maximum of 90 days.

PayPal buyer insurance

In addition to filing a claim at eBay, if you've paid for an item through PayPal and you feel a fraud is in the air, rush to file a complaint with the PayPal Buyer Complaint form.

It's crucial that you go through PayPal (rather than going directly to your credit card company). As I discuss in Chapter 8, PayPal handles claims made against sellers.

If you feel your situation is a case of fraud, and eBay agrees with you, you are also covered by PayPal's $200 additional coverage. Visit `www.paypal.com/cgi-bin/webscr?cmd=p/gen/protections-buyer-outside` for more information.

You can also click the Security Center link on the bottom of any page on the PayPal site.

SquareTrade buyer protection program

SquareTrade has a buyer protection program that provides fraud coverage in addition to the $200 provided by eBay and PayPal.

That means the entire group of programs may protect you, *if* you meet the eligibility guidelines.

Your coverage depends on the level of coverage each SquareTrade seal member applies for within his or her membership; the max is $550.

One caveat: It's quite unlikely that a SquareTrade seal holder is going to defraud you. SquareTrade checks sellers' feedback and reports on a daily basis to be sure they're playing within the eBay rules. SquareTrade yanks back its seal of approval if anything fishy appears to be going on.

Verified Rights Owner Program

Another reminder: eBay is a venue. It is a place where sellers sell their wares to smart shoppers like you. No one at eBay owns the items, and no one at eBay can guarantee that items are as described in auction listings.

That means that you could, theoretically, buy a "genuine" Kate Spade purse at eBay for $24, and immediately realize when it arrives that the purse is counterfeit . . . and that's *not* eBay's fault. It's not that eBay doesn't care, that's why the eBay Powers That Be instituted the VERO (Verified Rights Owner) program.

Shame on you for thinking you could get that kind of deal on a new Kate Spade purse (but if you can, e-mail me and let me know where).

Just because, technically, eBay doesn't take the blame for its fraudulent sellers' handiwork, doesn't mean that eBay doesn't care if you get duped. Seriously, the VERO program connects eBay with companies or persons that care to protect their intellectual property rights (such as a copyright, trademark, or patent), which could possibly be infringed by an eBay listing.

If the Kate Spade people register at eBay as a VERO member, they give eBay the right to end auctions that they find on the site to be questionable.

VERO members send proof to eBay that they own the specified intellectual property. In return, they can report infringements to eBay, and eBay's listing police will end the counterfeit listings. This is not an automatic service, and the property owners are responsible to find their own infringements on the site.

Many of the VERO members have their own About Me pages. To see a list of links to their pages go to `http://pages.ebay.com/help/community/vero-aboutme.html`.

Knowing What eBay Investigates

Although eBay encourages the community to police the site, it also does its own investigations. You're a beginner, so I'm going to stress the buying violations. Some of them are very easy to fall into — and I don't want you getting in trouble on your first transaction. For now, here's the short list of things that eBay will look into.

There are rules for buyers as well as sellers. If you are reported and found responsible for any of the below offenses, you may be subject to disciplinary action. Violations may result in the indefinite suspension of a user's account, temporary suspension, or a formal warning. (Brrrrr . . .)

Buyer violations

Here's the skinny on the kinds of buyer violations eBay looks into. Many of these violations go both ways. For example, if a seller e-mails you and offers to do a deal with you off the site, that's a violation from the seller's side. If another eBay member pulls any of these kinds of tricks with you, feel obliged to report him or her to eBay:

- ✔ **Transaction interference:** If anyone sends an e-mail to other buyers warning them away from a particular seller or merchandise, eBay will investigate.

- ✔ **Off-site purchases:** Contacting the seller and offering to buy (or sell) the item outside of eBay.

- ✔ **Invalid bid retractions:** Misuse of the bid retraction process is a serious eBay violation.

Every bid you place is a binding contract to buy. Even if eBay somehow didn't investigate you for retracting bids, the rest of the community would ostracize you — eBay members show no pity for serial bid retractors. (That's why bid retractions are listed on your ID card — see Chapter 5.)

- ✔ **Non-payment after winning an item:** If you bid or use the Buy It Now option, you must pay for your item. Again, not only does refusing to pay for items get you a scarlet letter, but it could result in your complete and total suspension from the eBay service. Forever. Period.

TIP

✔ **Unwelcome buyer:** If you bid or shop from a seller who clearly states terms that you do not fulfill, you'll be investigated. For example, Susie Seller can state in her item description that she refuses to sell to someone with negative feedback. If you have any negatives, then you shouldn't bid. If you do, and you win, you may be investigated.

If you really want the item, I suggest that you e-mail the seller and ask if you may bid on the item, even if you don't fulfill his or her terms — it never hurts to ask.

Another common example has to do with international shipping. Say Steve Seller says that he will only ship within the United States, and you live in another country. If you bid and win the auction, you may be investigated.

✔ **Bid shielding or shill bidding:** Using a secondary ID to illegally manipulate the price of an item, without any intention of ever paying for it, is verboten and will be investigated.

Finding the eBay life raft

Sometimes things happen, and you just don't know what to do about it. Maybe you have made a heinous mistake (who, me?), or you've seen something on the site that seems fishy. Who can you go to? Who's there to listen?

The Rules and Safety area of the eBay site has a support page where you may describe the problem using a series of drop-down menus. After using this system to explain your situation, you will usually get a response within 24-48 hours. The magic Web address for eBay's Rules and Safety support form is: `http://pages.ebay.com/help/basics/select-RS.html`.

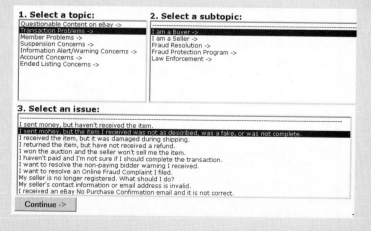

Where Else You Can Go for Support

I certainly think that eBay and the like give us plenty of places to go. But if things really get out of hand, you can go further to punish fraudulent sellers on your own.

Here's the list:

✔ **United States postal inspector:** If your deal involved the United States Post Office in any way, you can file a mail fraud complaint through the Postal Inspector's office. Your deal would involve the post office if you sent the seller payment through the mail and the seller sends you merchandise (or doesn't send at all) that is not what you ordered. To see the actual laws involved in mail fraud, go to www.usps.com/websites/depart/inspect/usc18.

Call (800) 275-8777 or your local post office for the required forms and information. After you file a fraud report, the USPS contacts the alleged bad guy on your behalf.

✔ **National Fraud Information Center:** The National Fraud Information Center is based in Washington, D.C. This organization collects reports of fraud and transmits the information to the National Fraud Database, maintained by the Federal Trade Commission and the National Association of Attorneys General. You can file your report online at www.fraud.org/info/repoform.htm or you can call (800) 876-7060.

The information you provide by filing a complaint with the NFIC informs federal and state regulators of potential illegal activities. It will not, on the other hand, get you your money back. By just reporting fraud, you can help prevent wrong-doers from victimizing others.

✔ **Local law enforcement agencies:** Contact the District Attorney or state Attorney General's office in the seller's city and supply as much information as these officers will take. You may also want to try the state's consumer affairs department — just run a Web search with the state's name and *consumer affairs*. Again, this option probably won't get you your money back, but may make you feel better.

✔ **FTC Bureau of Consumer Protection:** The Federal Trade Commission (FTC) Bureau of Consumer Protection runs a very popular Web site that takes complaints on fraud of all kinds. To file a complaint, go to https://rn.ftc.gov/dod/wsolcq$.startup?Z_ORG_CODE=PU01.

The FTC, in turn, works with many other leading crime prevention organizations. The FTC will send your information to all interested law enforcement organizations through its Web site: www.consumer.gov/sentinel/.

There's a good deal of solid information (some pretty scary information, as well) on this site. Check it out and help the good guys!

Internet service provider

As you know, every e-mail address ends with a @something.com or @something.net (or something like that). That something is the name of the person's ISP, or Internet service provider.

ISPs get very peeved when their users do illegal stuff online. Check out the ISP's Web site for fraud links, or try to report your issue to an e-mail address (usually, the address is something like fraud@ISPname.com). Let the ISP know that you have filed a complaint against one of its customers, explain the nature of the problem, and list the other agencies that you've contacted. They will usually take notice and may suspend the account of the company in question.

A very thin line separates alerting other members to a particular member's poor behavior and breaking an eBay cardinal rule by interfering with an auction. Feel free to hunt for facts, but don't point fingers on public message boards or chat rooms. If it turns out that you're wrong, you can be sued for libel.

Chapter 8

Ways to Pay for Your Stuff

*W*hen I talk to people about why they don't buy at eBay, one of the most popular answers is that they are afraid of giving out their credit card information. The second-most common reason is that they don't want to send money to strangers. In addition to all the eBay safeguards that I mentioned in previous chapters, here's the inside scoop on how to stay safe when sending your payment to the sellers. You'll be surprised to know that there are distinct levels of safety in how you can send payment to a seller.

I'm not going to discuss this at length. Just take my word for it. Do not send cash through the mail to anyone. Ever.

Paying with PayPal

PayPal is my preferred method of payment at eBay. I've been happily using PayPal since the company was first introduced to eBay, and I have always had positive results. Well, okay, not always. No service can make a slow or lazy seller into the picture of efficiency. The advantage of PayPal, though, is that you don't have to get your hands dirty.

For example, once, I had a problem with a slow-shipping seller and luckily I had paid him through PayPal. I filed a complaint through PayPal and I got my merchandise delivered within a day!

The fine people at eBay know a good thing when they see it, and the company acquired PayPal late in 2002; now PayPal payments are directly integrated it into eBay's checkout process.

Registering your data

First things first. It might be more convenient to register at PayPal, *before* you want to buy something. It's free and easy — and more convenient. Follow these steps:

1. **Go to the PayPal home page at** www.PayPal.com.

2. **Look for a link in the upper-right corner of the page that says** <u>Sign Up</u>**. Yep, that's right, click there.**

   Signing up for a PayPal personal account is a very simple procedure — one single page.

3. **Give your name, address, phone number, and e-mail address. You also have to make up a password.**

   Make your password more than six characters, and use numbers *and* letters! — revisit Chapter 1 for more information on registration security.

4. **Select a security question.**

   The safest is your pet's name, city of birth, or the last four digits of your Social Security number.

   Then you'll come to a security test. This is a special technology that prevents people from making continuous automated registrations on the site.

5. **Type the characters in the yellow box, as you see them (without any spaces).**

   Next, you'll be asked if you want a Premier Account. This may be something you want at a later date, but for now, unless you intend to sell, pass it by.

6. **Click in the box that says No.**

   You also have to click in the check box that indicates that you have read and agree to PayPal's User Agreement and Privacy Policy.

7. **When you're convinced that you understand what PayPal's all about and what it expects of you, click the button that says Sign Up.**

There are links so you can read all about PayPal. Feel free to click them.

PayPal sends you an e-mail confirming your registration. The e-mail arrives almost instantaneously to the e-mail address you used at registration, and it contains a link.

8. **When you receive the e-mail, click the link to visit the PayPal site.**

9. **Enter the password that was used to create your account.**

Bingo — you're in.

Giving PayPal credit card (or checking account) information

After you become a member of PayPal, you'll be asked to input a credit card to cover your purchases. That is, if you want to pay for anything with a credit card. It can be your choice — anything you wish from MasterCard, Visa, American Express or Discover.

If you don't have a credit card or would like to occasionally pay for things directly from your bank account, you'll have to register your checking account. Once you do, you can purchase things and debit your checking account for payment.

How your credit card company handles PayPal transactions

To be a good consumer, you need to take responsibility for your transactions; be sure you understand your credit cards terms and conditions when it comes to third-party payment services. Each credit card company has its own agreement with PayPal and each company has a different view on how to handle PayPal transactions. For example, Visa and MasterCard treat PayPal as the "Merchant of Record" in your transactions, meaning that PayPal ends up as the responsible party if you don't receive the merchandise or if you dispute the transaction. If you make a complaint about a charge made on your Visa or MasterCard, the credit card company just yanks the money from PayPal, and it's up to PayPal to settle things with the seller.

Because of the way credit cards deal with this kind situation, it is of utmost importance that if you have an issue with a seller, you report the seller *first* to PayPal! Do not go to your credit card company before contacting PayPal. PayPal will do its utmost to protect itself — and you — from being ripped off.

At the time of this writing, Discover and American Express treat PayPal transactions somewhat like a cash advance — a money transfer of sorts. I just checked a couple of my past Discover and American Express bills, and the PayPal charges look like any other charges. You can't tell the difference. The only difference is how these credit card companies handle their level of liability in third-party payment services.

This is the main reason PayPal backs up eBay's insurance (see Chapter 7) with $200 additional coverage (see "Giving PayPal credit card (or checking account) information" earlier in this chapter). This coverage is good for purchases up to $400.

I can see you beginning to squirm from here, you're not terribly comfortable giving that type of information to anyone, much less putting it out on the Internet. I'm very glad you feel that way, but relax. PayPal uses military-strength encryption technology to keep your account information safe, so don't be afraid to give up your data.

To register your credit card, you'll have to input the name on the card (the last name is already filled in with the name you registered on the account), the expiration date and the Card Verification number. The Card Verification number is the three-digit number on the back of the card, imprinted next to the card number in the area where you sign. PayPal also asks you to supply a billing address.

On an American Express card, the Card Verification number is the four-digit number on the right side of the face of the card.

When you enter all the information PayPal needs, click the Add button.

PayPal submits your information to your credit card company for confirmation. This process may take a minute or so, but eventually, your credit card company says that you are who you say you are; the card is added to your PayPal account. You can register four active credit cards.

Registering your checking account is just as easy. You supply the information from the bottom of one of your checks as shown in Figure 8-1.

Figure 8-1: Provide your bank routing number and your account number.

Getting verified

When PayPal has the information it needs, it makes two small deposits into that account. (When I say *small*, I mean small!). This is so that PayPal can verify that the bank account is yours. When you opened your account at your bank, you had to provide certain levels of identification. By verifying you with your bank, PayPal can check your identity as well. After a week or so, call your bank and find out the amount of these two deposits. When you have the amounts, sign in to the PayPal Web site, with your password, and type the amounts in the appropriate place and *voila,* your account is registered — and, not coincidentally, you're verified!

PayPal has confirmed that you hold an active account with your bank. All banks are required to screen their account holders, and verification authenticates your identity to anyone who does business with you.

Here are some benefits of being PayPal-verified:

✔ Verification increases your spending limit from $2,000 to *unlimited!*

(Uh-Oh!)

✔ Now you can register eight active credit cards instead of four.

(So you can reach unlimited $$ faster?)

✔ You're covered by PayPal's additional $200 fraud insurance.

(That's worth the trouble!)

If your eBay purchase qualifies for coverage under eBay's fraud protection plan (which I describe in Chapter 7) you are also covered for an additional $200 from PayPal when you purchase your item from a PayPal Verified seller. This is, provided that you are a verified buyer. (To see if a seller is verified by PayPal, look for a PayPal Verified icon in his or her eBay auction, as shown in Figure 8-2.)

Figure 8-2: Look for the PayPal Verified icon when selecting a PayPal seller.

Ways to pay through PayPal

The easiest and most efficient way to pay for eBay purchases is by credit card. If you are not a PayPal-verified buyer, you still have your credit card's fraud protection guarantee behind you.

You may also send money directly from your bank account (either savings or checking) through instant transfers or eChecks — as long as you have check writing privileges for the account.

- ✔ **Instant transfer:** An instant transfer is *immediately* debited from your bank account and deposited into the seller's account — so you'd best be sure you have the funds in your account to back up the purchase now (not tomorrow, not next week). PayPal requires you to back up an instant transfer with a credit card, just in case you've miscalculated your account balance.

    Find help for this type of transaction at www.paypal.com/cgi-bin/webscr?cmd=_help-ext&eloc=230&unique_id=01718&source_page=_home.

- ✔ **eCheck:** PayPal also lets you pay for your purchases with an eCheck, which is just like writing a check, only you don't write it with a pen. Like regular, plain-vanilla paper checks, eChecks take three to four days to clear, and do not post to the seller's account as paid until then.

Sellers will not ship your item until the eCheck clears, so if you're in a hurry, don't use this option.

Using PayPal's AuctionFinder

PayPal also has a service called AuctionFinder. Here's how it works. Say you've just won a bunch of auctions by different sellers, and you want to pay for them all at once. Okay, so visit the PayPal site and sign in.

After you sign in you're taken to your main account page. In the center of the page, you see your recent account activity. There will also be links to <u>All Activity</u>, <u>Auctions Won</u>, and <u>Auctions Sold</u>.

Click the <u>Auctions Won</u> link. PayPal searches the eBay site and finds all the auctions you've won at eBay that haven't been paid for by PayPal. See Figure 8-3 for a glance at the AuctionFinder.

You must click the link for every auction to be sure that the seller accepts PayPal because all current auctions you've won at eBay (until you pay them on PayPal or remove them from the Finder) show up on AuctionFinder.

On the PayPal AuctionFinder page, just click the Pay button and go through the payment process. Click the Remove button to exclude sellers who don't accept PayPal.

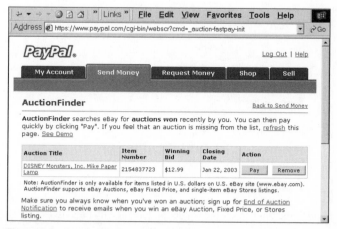

Figure 8-3: AuctionFinder on PayPal.

Making a PayPal Payment

After you win an auction, buy an item in a Buy It Now transaction, or purchase an item from an eBay store, it's time to pay. If the seller has a clickable link to PayPal, you can pay immediately by clicking the Pay Now icon, as in Figure 8-4, on the item page.

Figure 8-4: Pay now by clicking here when you want to pay for your item through PayPal.

After clicking the Pay Now icon, a second browser window opens, as shown in Figure 8-5. Double-check that all the purchase information is correct. If insurance is optional, and you don't want shipping insurance, just delete the amount.

Payment Details

PayPal is the authorized payment processor for **Wendy Warren** .

Pay To:	Wendy Warren
Payment For:	Kitty Kitten Cat Enamel Enameled Bracelet NEW
Quantity:	1
Your Auction ID:	veteran-shopper
Currency:	U.S. Dollars
Amount:	$9.99
Sales tax:	8.250% in CA
Shipping & Handling:	3.85
Insurance per item: (optional)	

If you have never paid through PayPal, Click Here

PayPal Login
Welcome, Marsha Collier!

Email Address:	marshac@collierad.com Problems logging in?
PayPal Password:	Forget your password?

Figure 8-5: Signing in to make your payment with PayPal.

Assuming that you've already become a registered (verified) PayPal user, you see a place at the very bottom of the page to input your e-mail address and password. Fill in this info, and then click the Continue button.

A page appears, and you must decide whether you want to pay by credit card or bank transfer. Finalize all the details of your transaction, by selecting your payment method in the Source of Funds area. The default (if you have no money from sales in your account) is an instant transfer of funds from your bank. If you prefer to use your credit card, be sure to click the <u>More Funding Options</u> link to change the payment method to your credit card. You can even send a note to the seller along with your payment.

Within moments of your payment, PayPal sends sellers an e-mail saying that it has received your payment. Although there is a place for you to leave a note for the seller, the note is buried in this much longer e-mail message that PayPal sends, and it's hard to find. If you want some information to go to the seller regarding your transaction, send the information in a separate e-mail message.

All important messages should be sent separately. Put the eBay item number in the Subject line.

Using Your Credit Card Safely

The safest way to shop at eBay is to use a credit card either directly through a secure site or through an online service such as PayPal. In most cases, your credit card company (or online payment service) will stand behind you (and refund your payment) if you encounter problems using your card online.

Debit cards and credit cards are two entirely different things. Companies will back your purchases on a credit card (remember that the credit card company gets a small percentage for its trouble) versus a debit card, which is actually a direct withdrawal from your checking account.

Knowing your credit card company's policy

First (before you start bidding), find out how your credit card handles fraud claims. (Check out Chapter 7 for more on avoiding and reporting fraud.) The major credit card companies — American Express, Discover, MasterCard, and Visa — all have different policies as to how they will stand behind you when it comes to online purchases:

- ✔ **American Express:** American Express offers "ironclad protection" for online shoppers. The company claims that there's "no fine print and no deductible" if you need to rely on American Express to help you fight a fraudulent transaction. Visit `www.americanexpress.com/cards/online_guarantee`.

- ✔ **Discover:** Discover offers 100 percent fraud protection. The company even offers free, downloadable software that generates a single-use card number. With this program, each time you shop online, your account number is never actually transferred over the Internet. Visit `www2.discovercard.com/simple_secure/fraudprotection.shtml`.

- ✔ **MasterCard:** The program offered by MasterCard is called Zero Liability, and is offered if MasterCard deems your account in good standing, you haven't broadcast personal account information online frivolously, and that you limit the number of unauthorized events you report each last year.

I believe it appears that MasterCard is the final judge when it comes to fraud, not you, so be careful. Be sure you document all your purchases by printing out the auction and all e-mails during and after the transaction. Visit `www.mastercard.com/general/zero_liability.html`.

- ✔ **Visa:** Visa seems to like the phrase *zero liability,* as well. Your liability for unauthorized transactions is $0. A new program, called Verified by Visa, lets you set up your own private password that you use with your Visa card any time you use it online, adding another layer of security to your transaction. Visit `www.usa.visa.com/personal/secure_with_visa/zero_liability.html`.

In addition to double-checking your statement every month, check your credit card company's Web site or call the credit card company's customer service department every once and a while to verify its current fraud protection policy for online purchases.

Never — really, I mean never *ever* — send your credit card information to anyone through e-mail. E-mail is the most insecure way to send information. As your e-mail makes its way from your computer to the recipient's desktop, it wends its way across the country making micro stops hither and yon along the way. These stops may take just nanoseconds, but your information is open for reading by outside parties (at least those who have the right expertise) at any stop along the journey.

Adding a layer of protection with an online checkout service

Many eBay sellers use an independent online checkout service that allows them to process shipping information, combine purchases, give an exact shipping total, and receive credit card payments. If the seller uses such a service, when you win the auction, you'll probably see a clickable link in the e-mail that's sent to you at the end of the auction. The link leads you to an online checkout page. There are many of these services on the site such as AuctionWorks, Channel Advisor and Zoovy. (See Chapter 2 for a demonstration of the third-party checkout process.)

Beware the money order

For the same reason that eBay sellers *love* money orders, you really have to be *excruciatingly careful* to whom you send money orders. The bottom line is that you are sending cash. A seller can cash a money order and "forget" to send you the merchandise you paid for. How could a seller possibly forget to send you something you paid for with your hard-earned money? Cash payment = no receipt. No receipt = no paper trail. No paper trail = no proof. No proof = seller amnesia. I'm not saying that sellers are dishonest. Most are very honest, especially the ones with a high feedback rating!

The only paper trail is the cashed money order, and unless it was cashed at a place where they actually know the payee (like the bank), the money order could have been stolen and cashed by someone else. For example, if you pay by money order, you have no recourse other than reporting problems to some federal agency about mail fraud. I'm sure that some nice government employee will happily take a report and sound very interested and sympathetic, but bottom line — you'll be out your money. Plus, you don't get the extra muscle that you get when a credit card company backs you up.

If your transaction falls within eBay's fraud protection policy, you'll be covered up to $200, but if not, you could be kissing your money goodbye. *Caveat emptor!*

Checking for sure signs of security

When you come to the point at any checkout online that requires that you input your credit card information, (see Figure 8-6) there are a couple of very important things to look for:

- ✔ **Be sure that the site that hosts the checkout is secure:** Look for icons in the lower-right corner in the status bar of your Internet browser (either a small closed padlock or a key).

- ✔ **Check for an s:** The URL (address of the Web site) may change from a prefix of `http://` to `https://` (the s stands for secure).

- ✔ **Look for an SSL:** You may also see the initials SSL in the Web site's address or somewhere on the page. SSL stands for Secure Socket Layer.

Any, some, or all of the above items indicate that the Web site uses security encryption methods. Translation? No one but you and the merchant can read or view your payment information.

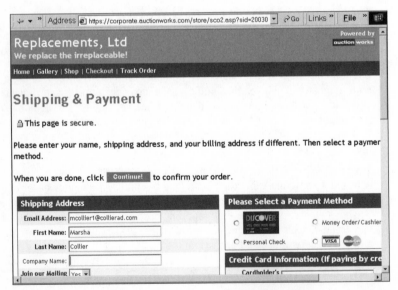

Figure 8-6: Secure Credit Card Checkout in AuctionWorks.com.

Sending Money Orders

Money orders are beloved by all eBay sellers! Even though PayPal is usually their first choice — because payment arrives almost instantaneously and sellers avoid having to track payments they're waiting for — money orders are a close second because they are just like cash.

Many hobbyist sellers just cash their money orders, or bring postal money orders with them to the post office to pay for postage. No fuss, no muss — no need to deposit the money order in the bank. Get it? *(Wink, wink.)*

You can purchase money orders at the post office in amounts up to $500, but, of course you have to pay a 90-cent fee. If you don't want to wait in line, convenience stores and supermarkets sell them for around $1. Don't waste your money and get a money order at your bank; money orders are a big profit item for bankers. The banks usually charge around $5 for the privilege of purchasing a money order!

 There's an online service called BidPay (www.bidpay.com) that's owned by Western Union (the venerable telegram people have come of age). BidPay can sell you a money order (charged to your credit or debit card) and mail it to the seller for you. BidPay charges $2.95 for money orders up to $30, and $5 for money orders up to $100. Amounts over $100 are 2.25% + $5.00. (This may seem like a pricey option, but you might find it useful if you're glued to your computer.)

Personal Checks

Personal checks are not a preferred method of payment by veteran sellers at eBay for many reasons. Let me explain why using an illustration:

> I sold a beautiful brand new Diane Von Furstenberg wrap dress (retail price $350 — an eBay bargain at $139!) to a lovely lady in the east. She sent me a check, which I immediately deposited. I waited 10 business days, which was my policy, and sent the dress on the 11th day. On the 12th day, the bank returned the check to me. Certainly this lady *knew* her check had bounced.

She *could* have e-mailed me to let me know, but she didn't. I called the buyer, and she sent a money order that covered both the check and my bounced check fees my bank charged me. But I didn't need the aggravation, and I was very lucky. Many sellers never get their money. Bounced checks can be a real problem for eBay sellers.

I'll give you a very important reason never to send a check to anyone when you shop at eBay. As a matter of fact, when you read my warning, you may never want to write a check in a store again. Take a glance again at Figure 8-1 in this chapter.

Remember that information on your check? Think about what someone might be able to do with that information and your home address. If someone really wants to, he or she also can get your phone number. And if you have your Social Security number on your check, (which you shouldn't) someone can practically set up shop as you!

Save yourself the trouble. Don't send out personal checks.

Part III
Searching eBay

"Just give me a few more seconds.
I'm about to make the winning bid
on this crib."

In this part. . .

The only way to get the best deals on the right items is to make sure that you find exactly what you're looking for before you bid. Part III shows you all the tricks to finding an item at eBay. Memorize a couple of tricks in these chapters, and you'll be shopping with savvy in a flash. And eventually, the search bug will hit you with such regularity that you won't even realize it. A case in point: While I was writing this introduction, I realized I was running out of a nutritional supplement that I use. I did a search for the product at eBay and bought it using the Buy It Now option. Before I finished typing the sentence you're reading, the product was ordered, the shipping was paid, and I had spent less money than I would have if I'd gone to the neighborhood health food store!

Chapter 9

Home: A Good Place to Start

In This Chapter

▶ Finding home page specials

▶ Clicking sidebar links

▶ Introducing the Navigation Bar

The best (and most sensible place) to begin your hunt for that special bargain is at the eBay home page. I like to think of the home page as an entrance to the future of shopping — no crowds to jostle you around, no lines to stand in, and no foolish clerks. No one looking over your shoulder, judging what you're browsing around for; no one saying, "*Those* golf clubs are for *pros,* we have *beginner's* clubs over here."

The eBay home page is neatly divided up into compartments that contain links to other parts of the eBay site. From here you can go anywhere, and until you are familiar with navigating the site, it's best to make this your point of entry.

There is an eBay logo on the upper-left corner of every eBay page. If you ever find yourself lost on the site and want to return to the home page, just click the word eBay to be transported back home.

Home Page Specials

The home page is sprinkled with small pictures that link to bargains and seasonal specials that are being featured throughout the site. Smack-dab in the center of the top of the page, eBay displays some special or timely sale items.

For example, at around Grammy time, the home page featured a charity auction that was tied in with the awards show (as shown in Figure 9-1). The organizers of the specials area want to make sure that eBay reflects what's going on in the world at the moment. It also wants to keep up with the trends so that members can find the deals of the day.

Featured auctions

One special area of the home page is the teaser for eBay's featured auctions (see Figure 9-2).

Featured auctions are fun to browse if you have the time. Sellers pay extra to have their auctions featured and linked to the home page for the extra exposure, but the auctions are also listed in eBay's categories. If you perform a search as described in Chapter 10, or browse the categories, as in Chapter 11, you won't miss these gems. eBay changes the links on a timed basis.

Figure 9-1: The eBay home page.

Featured Items

- South Dakota 80 Acres/Great Outdoors!/Cheap!
- Very Rare Hermes Kelly Bag. Only Five Made
- 100 Neon/100 Spiral Glow Sticks - Easter-Dutch
- $299 Leather Backpack Blow-Out Only $8.95!!
- *Little Packets Of Antique Wholesale Coins!*
- Greatest Hits Of The 60's - 8 Cd Set $14.88!!
- *all featured items...*

Figure 9-2: Featured auctions home page teaser.

Seasonal promotions

Further down the page, eBay lists seasonal specials that tie in with just what's hot — and what's selling that time of year (see Figure 9-3). Other times — say during ski season — eBay displays colorful graphics in this spot with links to bargains on ski equipment and deals on everything you'll need to make your ski vacation complete.

Figure 9-3: Fun and colorful home page promotions.

Sidebar Links

Along the left side of the home page, eBay displays links to major shopping areas of the eBay site. These are important links that don't change very often. The top section leads to eBay's specialty sites:

- ✔ eBay Motors (see Chapter 18)
- ✔ eBay Stores (see Chapter 15)
- ✔ Half.com (see Chapter 15)
- ✔ PayPal, eBay's payment service (see Chapter 8)
- ✔ Sothebys.com (see Chapter 15)

Below the specialties listings is a *very* abridged list of eBay's main categories. The home page has no room for the 18,000 or so category listings, so eBay lists the most popular main categories on the front page.

If you don't find the category you'd like to browse, you can go to the bottom of the list and click the link to <u>See All eBay Categories</u>. I give you more information on the categories in Chapter 11.

Below the listing of eBay top-level categories are links to some of eBay's special areas. You'll see a quick link to the Charity area (see Chapter 22) where sellers raise money for major charities. You'll also see the link to eBay's Live Auctions, a similar site to Sothebys. com. Unlike Sothebys.com, however, Live Auctions has live auctions from a large variety of bricks-and-mortar auction houses. You'll also see links to professional services so you can find outside contractors for your business and wholesalers (where you can find lots of great goods) if you ever decide to become a seller at eBay (see Chapter 17).

At the very bottom of the list is a list of links to eBay sites around the world. If you're a U.S. citizen, you have 12 million or so listings to choose from, but maybe that's just not enough. Good news — you can visit the 20 international sites. By the way, the international sites are a great place to practice your high school French — or Portuguese, Japanese, German — you get the idea.

Using the Navigation Bar

Because you enter eBay from the home page, I'd like to introduce you to something you will see consistently throughout the eBay site. There's a very handy item on the top of the home page (and every eBay page) that gives you links to navigate the eBay site. It's the Navigation Bar. This handy little tool is always there to help you out. I find that even though I'm very familiar with where eBay puts everything, I still use the Navigation Bar as a shortcut to get where I want to go on the site.

First, there's the line on the top of the Navigation Bar, which is the part I use the most:

✔ Click <u>Home</u> to get back to the home page.

✔ Click <u>My eBay</u> to get to your very own My eBay page, where you can track all your auctions and eBay transactions. (Read more about it in Chapter 4.)

✔ Click <u>Site Map</u> to see a page that has links to just about any place you need to go on the eBay site — without confusing, extraneous illustrations and text.

✔ Click <u>Sign In</u> to get to the sign in page, discussed in Chapter 2.

The eBay Navigation Bar doesn't stop there. When you click the individual boxes of the Navigation Bar, context-sensitive drop-down links to other places at eBay appear.

When you click the Browse button, a new page appears, and the Navigation Bar drops down with four additional boxes:

✔ Categories (that's the page you're on)

✔ Regions (see Chapter 15)

✔ Themes (see Chapter 13)

✔ Stores (see Chapter 15)

✔ Links to the Featured Auctions and Categories (see Chapter 11)

Clicking the Services button opens up one of six target pages. The most important pages for beginners are the Buying and Selling box and Rules and Safety pages. Everything else you need for now is accessible from Your My eBay page, which I cover in Chapter 4.

The Buying and Selling box links to a page that has answers to many questions, and the Rules and Safety area is eBay's hub for SafeHarbor, which I cover in Chapter 7.

The Search button brings you to the Search area, which I explore in Chapter 10. You can also get the contact information of other members who you do business with by clicking the Find Members button.

Click Help to visit eBay's pop-up help system. If you have a pressing question, try finding the answer there.

If you're looking for eBay's chat boards or member posting areas, click the Community button to see where all the warm and fuzzy stuff goes on.

Chapter 10

Taking Advantage of eBay's Search Functions

*A*nyone can find an *auction* at eBay. Finding *bargains,* on the other hand, requires some finesse. The key is learning how to search the site for the hidden deals. Just as understanding the categories is important, knowing how to work the search engine will help you find your item for the lowest price.

When you perform a search at eBay, the search engine looks through every one of the 10 million or so items up for sale on the site to find the exact keywords you're looking for.

It's very important that you know about the item you are trying to find. Using extra keywords can turn a search that yields very little into a search that's spot on.

Ace Tips to Keep in Mind before You Start

When searching at eBay don't forget the following:

> ✔ **Ignore capitalization of proper names:** eBay simply doesn't care whether you capitalize or leave words lowercased. eBay's search engine doesn't distinguish between caps and non-caps.

✔ **Don't use noise words:** *and, a, an, or,* or *the* are called *noise words.* In searches, these words are interpreted as part of your search unless you enclose them in quotes. Let's say we want to find items from the 1939 classic film, *Gone with the Wind.* If you type in the proper title, you won't get as many hits.

I got 1,592 hits from *Gone with the Wind,* and then 1,699, with a search for *gone wind.* Many sellers drop the noise words from their titles, so use as few keywords as you can to narrow your search.

✔ **Don't search just within specific categories:** Although a category-specific search further narrows down your results, narrowing your search means that you will miss a great deal of items. Take a look at the chapter on categories, Chapter 11 for more info.

Using the Item Search Hub

There are several ways to perform an eBay search. The easiest way for beginners (that's you, for now) is to go to the eBay search area. Go to the top of any eBay page and find the Navigation Bar, shown in Figure 10-1. Click Search.

Figure 10-1: eBay's Navigation Bar.

Use eBay's Search button on the Navigation Bar to perform three types of searches. You can

✔ Find items

✔ Find members

✔ Set up your favorite searches

Doing a basic search

When you click Search, you're faced with three options — you can search for items, members, or favorite items. You're probably looking for stuff, so click Find Items. A page like the one shown in Figure 10-2 appears.

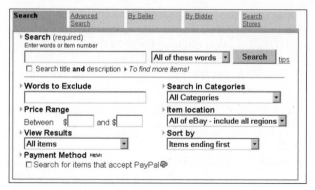

Figure 10-2: Start here to do a basic search.

This is the basic search form. You'll see the following areas in this form. You can fill out some or all of them. The more information you type into this form, the more narrow your search can be.

If you make your search *too* narrow, you may miss out on some real bargains. If you're looking for real bargains, incorporate the search tips from Chapter 3.

Stumped on what words to use in your search? Think of the item you are trying to find. Look at it and determine which words best describe it.

For example, select the brand name, color and descriptive words. Say your favorite china pattern has been discontinued; to search eBay for missing pieces in the set, follow this process:

1. Determine the manufacturer's name.

I'm looking for Dansk.

If you don't have all the information you need, check out the manufacturer's Web site, or a Web site that specializes in the collectible you're looking for.

2. Specify the series, collection, pattern, or design, as well.

Sometimes there is more than one. For example, I am searching for Bistro (the name of the collection) and Maribo (the pattern name).

3. Narrow your search even further, if possible or necessary.

For example, I need to replace a salad plate.

4. Enter the words for your search.

For example, type ***Dansk Bistro Maribo salad***.

If someone has listed some items with all those words in the title, we'll be lucky and pull up some winners.

It's likely that the words in your initial search are buried in the description.

5. **Click in the box that says Search Title and Description.**

This makes sure that information in the description is also lassoed by your search.

If that search pulls up too many auctions, you can always redo the search and search through the item titles only.

You see some tools to narrow down my search even further. For example, next to the typed in keywords, there is a drop-down box that allows you to tell the search engine to interpret your entry. The search engine can search the title and description for

- All the words

- Any of the words

- The exact phrase in the order it is written

6. **When you're ready, click Search.**

A list of auctions, in the order of when they close (soonest at the top) appears.

Refining even the most basic search

The search engine at eBay has become more sophisticated than ever. If you know an item number, you can type it in to any of eBay's search boxes throughout the site, and eBay's search takes you directly to that auction item.

In addition, you can choose other criteria:

- ✔ **Words to exclude:** If you're looking for some silver flatware, and you want it to be solid, not plated, at this point, you could type in **plated** so that your search would exclude an item listing that has the word *plated* in it.

- ✔ **Price range:** Here's where you can narrow down your search to a specific price range. You can type in a low and a high maximum amount that you're willing to spend.

Personally, I rarely use this option, and I don't recommend using it because you never know what you might miss. Just leave the boxes blank.

✔ **View results:** You can choose whether you want to see All Items with Item Number, or Gallery Items Only. Why? I'm not sure, I always want to see all the results I can, so I leave this on the default — All items.

✔ **Payment method:** Here you can check a box to find only items that accept PayPal. This sort of search would exclude any items that are selling for half or a quarter of the going price, and only take money orders. Thanks, eBay. But no thanks — show *all* the results if you want the best deal you can get.

✔ **Search in categories:** Here you can narrow your search to one of eBay's top-level categories. Nice idea if you know for sure where the item is listed. But that's a rarity because categories cross over so much. For example, dishware could be listed in Home & Garden, Pottery & Glass, or Antiques.

I suggest leaving this option alone so your search encompasses all categories.

✔ **Item location:** You can narrow the search so that the engine only looks at eBay's Local Trading regions. Great idea if you're looking for something too bulky to ship.

✔ **Sort by:** You can also sort the order you want your results to appear in. For example, if you want to check out auctions in order of how soon they're closing, choose Items Ending First.

This is my favorite option — who knows if you'll miss the deal of the century while you're sifting through hundreds of listings in another order.

If you conduct the same kind of search rather regularly, and are familiar with most of what is currently up for sale, you can sort by Newly Listed Items First.

Lowest Prices First and Highest Prices First list the results just as you guess they do.

Understanding the icons

When you are presented with your Search results, you may notice there are tiny icons next to some of the items. Here's a key to what those little pictures mean:

✔ **Golden yellow rising sun** picture means the listing is brand new — the icon stays on for the first 24 hours an item is listed.

✔ **A small camera** means the seller has included a picture along with the item description, and you must open the item listing to see the picture.

✔ **Flaming match** means the item is hot! hot! hot! and has over 30 bids on it.

✔ **Small blue gift box** means that the seller may perform gift services for that item, such as wrapping and shipping to another address.

✔ **A golden picture frame** may show up in a category search, indicating that the item is listed with a Gallery photo. Gallery photos are the small pictures of the item that you see next to a listing when you run a search.

✔ **Small powder blue paddle** indicates the item is being sold through a live auction. Click the item for more details.

Performing an advanced search

An advanced search (see Figure 10-3) brings your search into closer focus — it will narrow your search down even further than the basic search functions. All the same options are available here, plus a few extra.

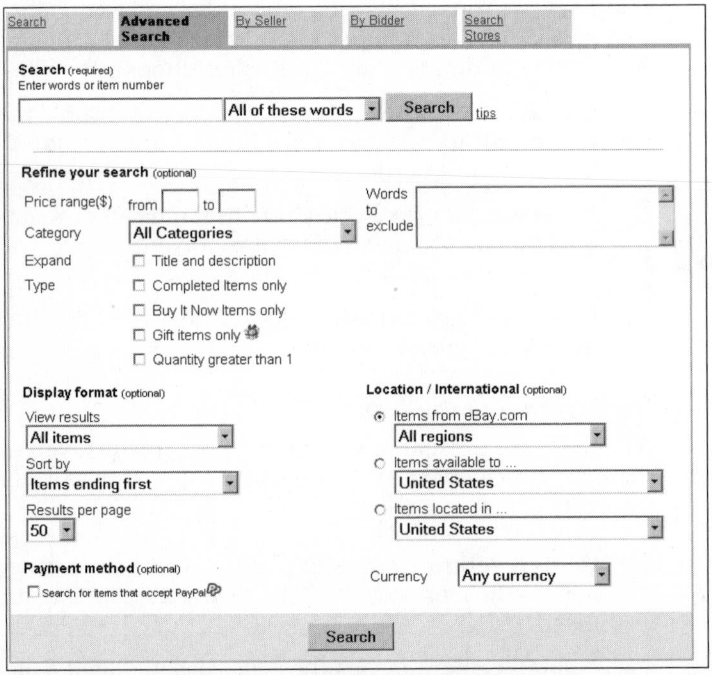

Figure 10-3: The second tab, eBay's Advanced Search.

They include

- ✔ **Completed items:** By selecting the completed option, you can research how often the type of item you're interested in has sold for within the past two weeks. This is a very handy tool, if you're not quite sure how much to bid for an item.

  Gone are the days of being able to really research an item by studying completed auctions with a title and description search. eBay now limits completed auction searches to title only. This can severely hinder your research ability.

- ✔ **Buy It Now items only:** This option comes in handy when you simply *must* purchase something immediately. The Buy It Now option would work well for the pair of tickets you've found to "The Producers" (when it hits your town). It could also be a great option when you're about to run out of your favorite moisturizer, and you don't have time to make it to the store within the next week to pick some up.

  When you look at your Search results, all Buy It Now items are very clearly marked, and can also be isolated by clicking the Buy It Now tab, as illustrated in Figure 10-4.

- ✔ **Gift items only:** Yee-ha! If you need an item that comes gift wrapped (and you don't want to see any other results), choose this option.

Figure 10-4: The Buy It Now tab on the Search results page.

If you want an item gift wrapped and sent to another party, always e-mail a seller ahead of time and make a request. If you have good feedback, most sellers will be more than happy to accommodate your gifting needs.

✔ **Quantity Greater than 1:** This can be a handy option if you're looking for multiples of a particular item. If you want more than one, it never hurts to ask a seller if he or she has more of an item. Very often sellers put additional items up for sale upon request.

✔ **International Searches:** You may also now narrow your search to items available to foreign countries.

Tricks to speed up your search

Item searches can be performed directly from any of the small search boxes that dot the eBay site. *There's one on almost every page!* In Table 10-1, there are a few abbreviations that I use to narrow down my eBay searches.

To speed up a search from pages other than the main Search page, I recommend memorizing the shortcuts in Table 10-1. You'll rarely, if ever, have to go to the eBay Search area to find an item again!

Table 10-1	Symbols for eBay Searches	
Symbol	*Impact on Search*	*Example*
No symbol, multiple words	Returns auctions with all included words in the title.	**olympus mount** might return an item for an Olympus camera, or an item from Greece.
"Term in quotes"	Search items with the exact phrase inside the quotes.	**"Stuart little"** is more likely to return items about the mouse than **stuart little** because it returns the words in the exact order you request.
Asterisk *	Serves as a wild card, good to use to include singular *and* plural of an item.	**budd*** returns items that start with budd, such as Beanie Buddy, Beanie Buddies, or Buddy Holly.

Symbol	Impact on Search	Example
Parentheses-enclosed words, separated without space, by a comma (a,b)	Finds items related to either item before or after the comma.	**(signed,autographed)** returns items with titles that have items that have been listed as either signed or autographed.
Minus sign −	Excludes results with the word after the −.	Type **signed-numbered**, and find items that are signed but not numbered.
Minus symbol and parentheses	Finds items with words before the parentheses but excludes those within the parentheses.	**enterprise -(poster,book)** means that enterprise items show up if book or poster is not in the title.
Parentheses	Searches main word plus both versions of the word in parentheses.	**political (pin,button)** searches for political pins or political buttons.

Searching for items by seller

After spending time at eBay, you'll find that you have favorite sellers. You can always access a seller's other items for sale by clicking the <u>View Seller's Other Items</u> link on the auction page.

The best place to keep track of your favorite sellers is on your My eBay Favorites page (see Chapter 4).

If you'd like to see if a seller has sold an item in the past that's similar to one you're interested in, the seller's search will come in very handy (see Figure 10-5).

To search for a seller's items, you merely have to type his or her e-mail address or User ID in the Single Seller box.

You can choose to see the seller's current auctions or the completed sales along with the current auctions. Just check the appropriate box before you conduct the search. You can also select the display order of the items and the number of items you'd like to see on the results.

If you have a group of sellers who you like to shop with who carry a similar group of items, you can always use the multiple seller search.

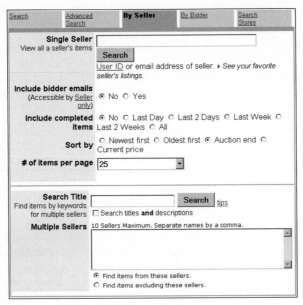

Figure 10-5: eBay Seller's search page.

You can use the multiple seller search to exclude up to 10 sellers from your search results. Click in the Find Items Excluding These Sellers option box. This function can come in handy if you've done business with someone in the past who you don't want to do business with again. Why repeat an uncomfortable situation?

Doing a bidder search

You may wonder, "Why would I want to run a bidder search?" Well, when you've been outbid by the same person several times, you might not need to ask that question.

If you want an item badly enough, you'll become very interested in the bidding patterns of others. (See Chapter 3 for more bargain shopping secrets.) Figure 10-6 shows eBay's Bidder Search page.

When researching your competition, always check out the bidder's completed auctions as well as the times he or she has been outbid. This will give you a complete grasp of his or her bidding *modus operandi*.

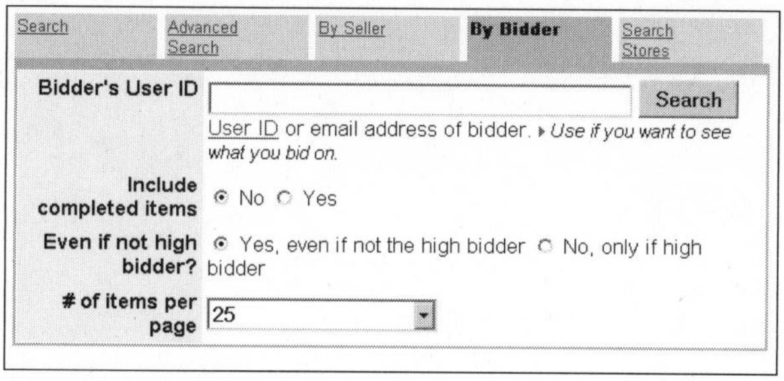

Figure 10-6: eBay's Bidder Search.

Searching the stores

The last tab of the eBay search area is the Search stores tab. It works exactly in the same way as the eBay Search tab. Remember that the inventory at eBay stores is not accessible from the eBay search engine, and you *must* search stores separately to find all the items that may interest you.

At the bottom of the Stores search is a Search by Store name box. If you can remember a portion of a previously visited eBay store name — you may be able to find it here. For the lowdown at eBay stores, visit Chapter 15.

Finding Other Members

The second drop-down box from the eBay Navigation Bar allows you to find information about eBay members. When you click the Find Members box, you can check out the User ID history of another member, as well as get his or her contact information.

To get contact information on another eBay member, you must be in (or have previously been in) a transaction with that member. You'll have to input the transaction number and the User ID of the other member. If eBay's computer sees that the two of you are involved in a transaction, your name and phone number will be sent to the other party, and you will be sent theirs. Getting this information is very helpful if you've run into a snag while closing an eBay transaction.

Chapter 11

Understanding eBay's Category Hierarchy

*U*nderstanding eBay's categories was a lot easier when there were just a few. I remember thinking that the quantity of categories was daunting when the site boosted the number up to the unthinkable 4,000. Now that the total number of categories is approaching the 20,000 mark, the time has come to either abandon all hope of understanding them, or to take things in hand and appreciate the elegance and organization of a system that's just beyond the realm of comprehension. You may never totally understand the category structure, but that's okay — what's important is knowing which categories sellers use most frequently.

As I write this book, eBay is adding, combining, and subtracting categories every two weeks to simplify the category structure. eBay works very hard to keep the site in an organized fashion; however, the constant reorganizing that's necessary can be a little daunting for new users. Don't worry.

How the Structure Works

Go ahead; ask me what I'm interested in. Let's see, I like art, golf, photography, fashion — I won't bore you with the rest, but it sounds like a fairly benign list, doesn't it? I'm sure your list of interests is the same. Straightforward, right?

So many categories!

Argh! Why so many? The bottom line is that the system was devised to make things easier for eBay members. The auction site started with some basic categories. Trust me; if eBay doesn't open up new categories to accommodate listings, you'd be complaining that the listings are impossible to browse.

Well, not quite. Say you like golf as much as I do. You might just click on the Sports category link on the home page, figuring you'll find Golf on the next page as a link.

Surprise! The Sports category is made up of approximately 2,700 sub, sub-sub, and sub-sub-sub categories of everything from golf balls to Pittsburgh Penguins jerseys. This organization wasn't created to confuse you. It's just that there are so many areas that your sports interest might take you. To accommodate the countless auctions that sports aficionados, collectors, and participants, list, eBay had to create a lot of small areas.

To keep your eyes from glazing over in awe, I've selected one of the smaller categories, Art. I only say small because the number of sub-categories can fit on one page — quite a feat these days. Figure 11-1 shows you how Art is divided up at eBay.

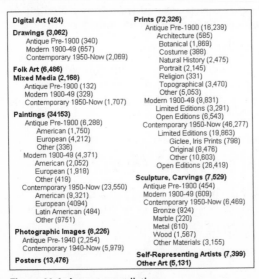

Digital Art (424)
Drawings (3,062)
   Antique Pre-1900 (340)
   Modern 1900-49 (657)
   Contemporary 1950-Now (2,069)
Folk Art (6,486)
Mixed Media (2,168)
   Antique Pre-1900 (132)
   Modern 1900-49 (329)
   Contemporary 1950-Now (1,707)
Paintings (34153)
   Antique Pre-1900 (6,288)
     American (1,750)
     European (4,212)
     Other (338)
   Modern 1900-49 (4,371)
     American (2,052)
     European (1,918)
     Other (419)
   Contemporary 1950-Now (23,550)
     American (9,321)
     European (4094)
     Latin American (484)
     Other (9751)
Photographic Images (8,226)
   Antique Pre-1940 (2,254)
   Contemporary 1940-Now (5,979)
Posters (13,476)

Prints (72,326)
   Antique Pre-1900 (18,239)
     Architecture (585)
     Botanical (1,869)
     Costume (388)
     Natural History (2,475)
     Portrait (2,145)
     Religion (331)
     Topographical (3,470)
     Other (5,053)
   Modern 1900-49 (9,831)
     Limited Editions (3,291)
     Open Editions (6,543)
   Contemporary 1950-Now (46,277)
     Limited Editions (19,863)
       Giclee, Iris Prints (798)
       Original (8,476)
       Other (10,603)
     Open Editions (26,419)
Sculpture, Carvings (7,529)
   Antique Pre-1900 (454)
   Modern 1900-49 (609)
   Contemporary 1950-Now (6,469)
     Bronze (924)
     Marble (220)
     Metal (610)
     Wood (1,567)
     Other Materials (3,155)
Self-Representing Artists (7,399)
Other Art (5,131)

Figure 11-1: Art category listings.

Figure 11-1 shows you the organized form of the main category, Art. The numbers in parentheses next to the sub-categories is the number of items that were up for sale in that category at the time I made the chart — I thought you'd find that interesting, and meaningful.

Drilling Down to Your Item

Depending on what you're looking for, things can get confusing. For example, say you want to find a category with items relating to your dog (maybe even a somewhat obscure breed, like a Schipperke) you might think you've got it made. I mean, how could a category for such an esoteric breed of dog be anything but very simple?

Schipperkes have their own category in the main category of Collectibles at eBay. (eBay has categories for over 80 breeds of dogs in Collectibles.) Currently there are three Schipperke items listed in the breed's own category.

But there are more auctions. When I ran a title search on *Schipperke*, I came up with 101 items. When I checked the little box to include descriptions, I got 124 listings. When I followed my own advice (see Chapter 10) and entered a search for *schipperk**, I found 129 items. When I searched for *shipperke* (misspelled), I found two more.

Items for Schipperke (and its misspellings) were listed in all these categories:

> Collectibles: Animals: Dog: Schipperke
>
> Collectibles: Animals: Dog: Other Dogs
>
> Collectibles: Animals: Dog: Corgi
>
> Collectibles: Animals: Dog: Poodle
>
> Collectibles: Animals: Dog: Doberman Pinscher
>
> Collectibles: Animals: Dog: Greyhound
>
> Collectibles: Animals: Dog: Labrador Retriever
>
> Linens, Fabric & Textiles: Kitchen Textiles
>
> Postcards & Paper: Postcards
>
> Books: Antiquarian & Collectible: Antiquarian

Books: Antiquarian & Collectible: First editions

Books: Nonfiction: Animals & Nature: Pets & Pet Care: Dogs

Books: Other

Books: Magazines & Catalogs: Magazines Back Issues

Home & Garden: Pet Supplies: Dogs: Other

Home & Garden: Pet Supplies: Dogs: Apparel

Home & Garden: Pet Supplies: Dogs: Grooming & Health Care

Home & Garden: Home Decor: Pillows

Art: Mixed Media

Art: Sculpture, Carvings

Business & Industrial: Printing Equipment: Presses: Heat, Transfer

Business & Industrial: Printing Equipment: Supplies, Consumables

Clothing & Accessories: Men: Casual Shirts

Clothing & Accessories: Women: Misses

Sothebys.Com: Prints: Modern Media

I hope you realize where I'm going with all this. Even though I picked a rather arcane item to search for, searching only through its designated category would have impacted your search significantly. You would have missed some of the more interesting items. Sellers make the decision as to where *they* think their items should be listed. If you ever meet me, ask me how I managed to (successfully, I might add) list an alcohol breath-tester key chain in the Barbie category.

If you're looking for a specific item, use eBay's search. Browsing through categories can be fun — if you have nothing special in mind.

Part IV

Shopping for Specific Items

The 5th Wave   By Rich Tennant

"Oh, we're doing just great. Philip and I are selling decorative jelly jars at eBay. I manage the listings and Philip sort of controls the inventory."

In this part. . .

Part IV gives you an idea of the millions of things that are sold on eBay. Believe me, you can find stuff you haven't even dreamed of yet. I read some of this information to some old-time eBay buyers and sellers, and even *they* were shocked! Who knew that you're just a mouse click away from buying blue-ribbon winning cookies?

Chapter 12

One-Stop Shopping for Family Fun

I used to think (as maybe you do, too) that eBay was great for all kinds of hand-me-downs for the family (okay, for the kids). Since I've made it my own personal shopping emporium, I've found unbelievable ways for a family to save money.

Of course, there are the obvious items. eBay allows you to get your hands on more used merchandise than you can possibly use, and there's no sin in getting used merchandise for certain occasions. But running a family provides innumerable less-obvious ways to spend money. In this chapter I show you how to be creative and save money at eBay.

Bringing Up Baby at eBay

Does it always seem that there's a baby shower when you have the least amount of time to go out and buy a present? And if you have a lot of friends (or a lot of kids), the amount of money you can spend on baby stuff can be astronomical.

Okay, perhaps the way I look at buying stuff for the kids at eBay doesn't reflect everyone's, but there was a time when my outlook was different. When my daughter was born, I certainly would have loved getting a brand new crib and mattress for half the retail price (including shipping). Actually, I think I would have gone for one of the used, expensive Italian designer cribs at eBay — they cost up to $700 in the real world (new), but at eBay they can be had for a couple hundred dollars.

Cribs aren't all you can get — just check out Figure 12-1. Here's just a sample of baby stuff you can find at eBay and have delivered to your door:

- ✔ Bassinets (search the misspelling *bassinete* for more items!)
- ✔ Diaper bags (see Chapter 14 for diaper coupons)
- ✔ Nursery furnishings — both new and used
- ✔ Carriages and strollers
- ✔ Clothes

The truth is that adorable designer baby clothes get worn for one picture (if you're lucky) before being outgrown and given away. (Or they get sold at eBay!) This fact also holds for those basically useless but lovely silver items that we like to give as baby gifts! You can find them brand new (in the box) selling for about half what you'd pay in the store.

- ✔ Baby seats

I've bought four top-of-the-line baby seats as gifts, and I haven't ever set foot in a baby store. I also had them mailed directly to the recipients so I didn't have to drag the big box to the party.

Figure 12-1: A bargain on a top-of-the-line Peg Perego high chair from seller, *babesntots.*

Helping the Kids Through School

Whether children are in a public school, private school, or being home schooled, they always need *stuff* for school. Lots and lots of stuff! When you're buying things, it seems like the list is endless. The older they get, the more expensive the stuff kids need becomes. Table 12-1 gives you an idea of just a few of the things my daughter needed for school.

These prices do not include shipping — so be sure to check how much the seller is charging for shipping before you bid.

Table 12-1	School Supply Bargains at eBay	
Product	**Street Value**	**eBay Price**
Jansport bookbag	$34.95	$14.99
Nike Shox shoes	$110	$49.99
TI Graphing calculator	$130	New $59; like new $20
100 #2 pencils	$15	$3.99

There are plenty more items at eBay — just give your item a chance and search!

Textbooks for home school, high school, and college

Textbooks are the most expensive items parents purchase. Many schools across the country have been faced with budget cuts, and parents must buy supplemental books for their children — even if the children attend public schools. Home schooling is becoming increasingly popular, and of course, parents need the appropriate books. Last of all? My daughter is in college; some of her used books cost more than $100 each — I don't even want to discuss the prices of the new books!

School and college bookstores buy back students' books at the end of the term — *maybe*. Maybe, because professors may decide to change books, or a new edition may be published. Then you're stuck with an expensive doorstop — er, textbook. But even if the bookstore does buy back copies of books at the end of the term, the bookstore only pays you a fraction of what you paid for the book in the first place.

Half.com

eBay acquired Half.com in July 2000. Half.com started as a person-to-person book sale site. In true eBay style, the site began to carry all types of items (other than books).

If you're lazy like me, you like to do all your shopping all in one place. Currently, you have to leave the eBay site in order to shop for stuff from Half.com. However, eBay just announced that Half.com will be fully integrated into the eBay platform by 2004. When the transition is complete, the Half.com site will disappear completely, and all the functions will be available within eBay.

I'm hoping that Half.com will remain a great way to buy books. In the meantime, if you go to Half.com (www.half.com or click the Half.com by eBay link under Specialty Sites on the eBay home page) you'll arrive at the page in Figure 12-2.

Turn over this book and look at the number above the bar code on the back cover. That's the ISBN (International Standard Book Number). Every book has an ISBN number, and if you type the ISBN number in the search box on the Half.com home page, listings for the book appear.

Figure 12-2: The Half.com home page with an ISBN ready to search in the book area.

Get your student's booklist and run the ISBN numbers through Half.com (or search the title through eBay). You'll save a bundle on books.

The cheapest way to ship books is using Media Mail rate. Using this method can take as long as two to four weeks to get across the country so do your online book shopping as early as possible. That is, unless you're saving enough money at eBay to pay for Priority Mail shipping!

For the junior musician

Way back in the olden days, when I was in high school, schools supplied musical instruments for the kids in band or orchestra to play. This is not so common an occurrence these days. Okay. I'll be honest: It never happens. Parents usually have to cough up an instrument for junior to play.

I didn't believe it myself, but eBay's musical instruments are cheaper (ahem, less expensive) than anywhere else on the planet. You see, if you buy a used instrument, you don't have to pay the middle man. Just like books, when parents sell the old instruments back to stores, the parents get pennies, and the stores polish up the instruments and sell them to another customer for just below the retail price.

Bricks-and-mortar-based music stores, like Musiqueweb (whose saxophone is featured in Figure 12-3), have found an excellent niche at eBay for their special instruments. Other sellers have opened eBay stores listing hundreds of beginner's instruments for sale.

The eBay site is also loaded with the miscellaneous accessories that playing an instrument requires. From sheet music and reeds to rosin, strings, and mouthpieces, eBay is the place to look for accessories, all at a discount.

I played violin in school, and I really miss it. So I recently bought a stunning, cherry red Yamaha electric violin at eBay for 40 percent less than I could have bought it for at the local music shop. I also bought sheet music with CDs that play the rest of the orchestra so that I'm not the only instrument playing. I can't wait till I have the time to really enjoy it!

Yanagisawa Solid Silver Alto Saxophone..FINE!

This is the famed Yanagisawa model A-9937 Solid Silver Alto Saxophone. This horn is a Music Convention demo horn. Hand picked to show to music educators. It was unboxed, shown for 3 days during the show and now we have it to sell at a great deal!!! One horn only..one great deal. Deluxe Yani case and mouthpiece included. Fully warranted to you, the original purchaser. No scratches, dents or dings....NEW.. Retail price is $ 12,400.00!!! .Here is info from Leblanc's site; A-9937 Featuring the same mechanical improvements as the A-991 artist series saxophones, the remarkable sterling silver A-9937 model takes its place among Yanagisawa's current top-line.

Figure 12-3: A saxophone even Lisa Simpson would love to play.

Don't forget to check out eBay Stores for your musical needs. Simply conduct a search (see Chapters 9 and 10) and look in the lower-left corner of the Search Results page that appears to see related eBay stores. Search stores also from the Search page on the Search Stores tab.

My Big, Bloated eBay Wedding

There's not a more bloated, high-maintenance event than a wedding. Where else do you face spending $1,200 for the cake alone? The expenses for a wedding never end. Just when you think you've got it all covered, you get the bill for 4 pounds of Jordan almonds (for some reason you can't have a wedding without 'em). When parents face a wedding (very often just after recovering from the college tuition nightmare) they will be very happy to know there are major savings to be had at eBay.

Searching the Everything Wedding theme page

Perhaps your eBay wedding *can* be original! When putting together a wedding, eBay's Wedding theme page can be a great help. You go to the Navigation Bar, click Browse, and then when the lower sub-Navigation Bar pops up, click Themes.

On the eBay Themes page (see Figure 12-4), scroll down to Weddings, and you'll find links to eBay searches that cover just about everything for a wedding!

Figure 12-4: The eBay Wedding theme page.

If you're serious about planning your wedding, Table 12-2 gives you a few search hints that eBay didn't put on the Wedding theme page.

Table 12-2	Wedding Searches
Search Term	*Number of Hits I Got*
wedding (gown,dress)	4,194 items
new wedding (gown,dress)	Narrowed down the search to only 823 items
wedding invitations	189 items for custom invitations
catering	224 listings for catering items (some were even gift certificates from caterers)

It looks like an eBay wedding

I found a lot of 10 bridal gowns at eBay that were being auctioned by the Making Memories Breast Cancer Foundation. I won all 10 gowns at a very reasonable price, with the idea of reselling them at some point (for a healthy profit — I do have a daughter in college, you know). These beautiful new gowns were donated to the charity by bridal shops and manufacturers around the country — so that it could resell them for cash. See Chapter 22 for more on great bargains that help charities.

My stepdaughter called a few weeks ago to announce that she's getting married. For a couple of weekends, she and her mother went from bridal shop to bridal shop and were very frustrated — until I told her about the gowns I bought at eBay. Well, no more worries about a bridal gown. Not only did she love one of the dresses I picked up, but it fit her perfectly.

When I ran my wedding gown search, I was shocked to see brand new, $1,200 wedding gowns selling at eBay for $200. That certainly leaves plenty of your budget to have the dress altered to fit the bride like a glove.

Wedding auction categories

You can find more than a couple of useful wedding categories at eBay to do your shopping. Remember that the first category listed is the main category, and it sifts down to the sub-categories:

- ✔ **Clothing & Accessories⇨Wedding Apparel:** This category includes shoes, accessories, bridesmaid dresses, and gowns.
- ✔ **Everything Else⇨Gifts & Occasions⇨Wedding Supplies:** This category covers wedding cake toppers, candles, favors, flowers and garlands, invitations, napkins, plates, ring pillows, pew bows, guest books, and the ever popular tulle.

Vacations Made Easy and Fun

Plan a vacation easily and reasonably at eBay. Aside from the time-shares (if you want to buy one, see Chapter 19) for rent in the most exotic locations, you can go to the Travel category and find lots of all-inclusive trips. These can be last-minute bargains from travel agents (make sure that the travel agency is registered with the (International Air Transport Association), or even from airlines.

Finding air travel bargains

You can also get bargains on air travel at eBay. Many people sell their *transferable* upgrades and reward tickets. I've found that a search for *fare upgrade* within titles and descriptions always nets a great deal of these certificates for sale at eBay. Also, a search for *airline ticket* yields lots of bargains.

Be sure if you buy an airline ticket at eBay that you ask all questions *first*. Are there restrictions on the ticket? An expiration date? Blackout dates? Also, if you know which airline your ticket is for, the deal may be safer because you can find all the airline's rules and regulations before placing a bid.

Many airlines say that vouchers, bonus discounts, and the like may be transferred, but not sold. To get these items at eBay, sellers get a bit creative. For example, the actual auction may be for an envelope, but the winner will also get the airline tickets for free (see Figure 12-5).

Sticker &
FREE Southwest Airlines R/T
Ticket
You are bidding on a really cool "Keep America Flying" sticker that was given to passengers who flew Southwest on the days following September 11. The winning bidder will also receive a *FREE SOUTHWEST RAPID REWARDS AIRLINE TICKET* (expires 08/16/02) that can be used for ONE ROUND TRIP or TWO ONE-WAY TRIPS anywhere Southwest Airlines files. Visit www.southwest.com to see cities served. This ticket is FULLY TRANSFERABLE and EASY TO USE and **remember you are bidding on the sticker and the airline ticket is FREE.**

Figure 12-5: A sale for a Southwest airline sticker (with a free roundtrip ticket).

Reining in restaurant bargains

I love finding restaurant deals at eBay. I tried the idea last year for the first time when I was planning a trip to Miami Beach. Just playing around, I searched *restaurant miami beach* (including titles and descriptions) and I came up with a bunch of restaurant gift certificates. I should say off the bat that I am not a big fan of coupons, and I always wonder about those restaurant discount booklets, but these auctions were going so cheaply I decided that making a bid was worth the risk.

I was going to Miami Beach for a week, so I bought six $25 gift certificates to various restaurants in the area that I was staying in. The winning bid price for these auctions was between $4 and $8. Let me say this again, for emphasis: I spent $4–$8 per $25 gift certificate. Basically, the way I think of it, I was being paid to eat out.

Well, I'm a believer now. Son of a gun, when I presented the certificates, each restaurant was happy and pleased to redeem them (even the very ritziest). Restaurants.com was the seller in all my Miami Beach restaurant coupon experiments. Currently, this eBay seller has close to 9,000 restaurant gift certificates for sale. The certificates are wonderful for everyday use and make great gifts, as well!

Getting Disability Resources

Many families deal with the hardships that accompany a family member's disability or decreased mobility. Whether the disability is the result of illness or injury, the loss of freedom can be difficult for everyone. And items that increase mobility and quality of life are expensive, hard to find, and, often, not covered by insurance. eBay offers a worldwide marketplace for special items for different disabilities.

My mother had macular degeneration. I only wish I'd had access to the glasses sold by the seller *annlarr@sympatico.ca* in Figure 12-6. I made a couple of searches to find it: *"legally blind"* (in titles and descriptions) and *macular* before I came across this auction.

Aside from searching a particular disability, try visiting the category Everything Else⇨Health & Beauty⇨Medical, Special Needs. You can find all kinds of items in this category, and the variety of listings is growing daily.

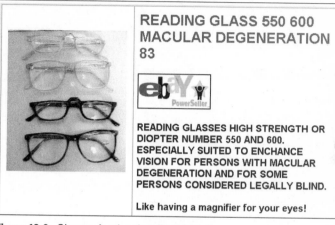

Figure 12-6: Glasses for the visually disabled.

Chapter 13

Finding Home and Garden Bargains

- -

In This Chapter

▶ Finding cooking supplies

▶ Finding outdoor supplies

▶ Getting sports equipment

▶ Meeting your holiday decorating needs

- -

Shopping at eBay for almost everything else makes sense. But after all, how can a Web site *really* help organize your home? When it's spring time, everyone likes to go outside, and no one wants to waste time inside on the computer! But what if you could go out and enjoy the crisp spring air while the mailman delivers all your spring home needs to your door?

This convenience makes even more sense in the winter. Why drive through snow and ice from store to store to find everything you need to make your *home* a more comfortable refuge?

Get Cooking!

What would eBay possibly have to share for your home life in the cooking area? Sure, you can get some great deals on pots and pans, but that's just scratching the surface! I bet you've flipped through a high-price kitchen appliance catalog or two in your day, and slobbered over some expensive must-have kitchen implement that you figured you wouldn't be able to find anywhere else.

Here's a great example: I have been coveting some elegant 18/10 stainless steel professional dish racks in catalogs. These babies sell for between $100 and $150 (not including shipping). While writing this book, I bought one of those very fancy-looking racks (brand new!) from an eBay seller for approximately $50 — including shipping! (Yay!)

Well, you can find just about anything at eBay if you look hard enough, and everything is available at a great savings. Just do a little search at eBay for *Pottery Barn* or *Williams Sonoma.* One recent search of mine (a simple title search for *Williams Sonoma*) netted a total of 709 items. You can find everything from new commercial baking pans to half-price, new hem-stitched napkins.

Items are marketed differently in different sections of the country. What goes on sale in Dallas may not go on sale in Oklahoma City. The Dallas eBay seller may buy a bunch of an item at a deep discount and put this sparkling new merchandise up for sale at eBay.

Getting hard-to-find recipes

Not only is finding unique recipes a no-brainer at eBay, but if you're not wealthy (or not a gourmand), many recipes are inexpensive and easy to prepare.

If you search for recipes, you'll come up with the expected number of recipe books, but as you skim the listings you may be surprised by what you'll find. For example, I did a little search for *recipes grandma* and came up with 355 unique items. Many were homemade compilations of original recipes that had been passed down through the generations.

Many sellers who use eBay as a venue put together their recipes in an eBook format that installs easily on your computer, or type in their recipes in a Microsoft Word file that they send electronically (upon payment, of course) via e-mail.

I'm not talking about one or two recipes here. I'm talking about hundreds of home cooking recipes for just a couple of dollars. (So much for granny's "secret" fried chicken recipe — I just bought it at eBay for $3 along with 299 other down-home southern recipes.)

Toss the word *charity* into your recipe search, and you'll be surprised at the amount of cookbooks that are available from Junior League, community organizations, and charitable organizations.

Also, finding some of the more, er, *esoteric* recipes is a snap. I ran a search for *French Normandy recipes.* I turned up with 22 items that varied from videos to books to eBooks. Now I know how to cook snails. Super.

I put together a small eBook of 23 original French Normandy recipes from a cookbook written (and published) by my great aunt in England. Buyers just get the file via e-mail, and it installs on their computer. Twenty-three great recipes delivered to your mailbox for only $5 — not too shabby! (Check out Figure 13-1.)

Finding foodie faves fast

As part of my research for this chapter, I ordered two 18-inch New York–style pizzas from an eBay seller. (The *sacrifices* I make for my readers!) The seller was *auctionsflyingpizzas.* This seller just opened an eBay store, and it already has impeccable feedback. The pizzas were packaged uniquely and arrived within a day. When put in the oven and resuscitated, they were admittedly, the best cheese pizzas my family had tasted. What a fun thing to send someone as a gift!

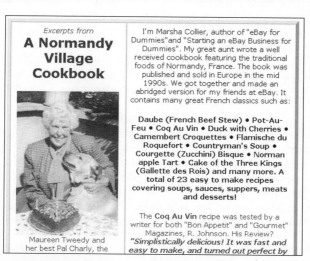

Figure 13-1: Aunt Maureen's abridged cookbook at eBay — sans escargots.

The pizzas I got from *auctionsflyingpizzas* weren't the first food items I got through eBay. I'm absolutely hooked on the chocolate truffle bars sold by seller *rejinsf* (see Figure 13-2). These babies are absolutely delicious and fresh. I've sent these truffles as gifts to friends (and gobbled them up with my family at home).

Artistic Hand Painted Chocolate Truffle Bar
Hand Painted Chocolate - "Banana Honey and Caramel"

"This is the best chocolate you'll ever taste." A Hand painted truffle with contrasting tiers of milk chocolate flavored with banana liquors, white chocolate infused with caramel, and dark chocolate and a hint of honey layered into a fanciful shape and hand painted with decorative colors and patterns.

Figure 13-2: Custom chocolate truffle bars for $9.95.

Many gourmet cooks who also happen to be computer-savvy entrepreneurs have begun to sell their specialties at eBay. With the advent of overnight and second-day shipping, many home-made, gourmet items can arrive at your door fresh and delicious. The best part is that you can read the feedback about what the food item tastes like *before* you order — I never would have tried the cabernet-wine soaked fruit cake last Christmas if I hadn't!

Also, if you know anyone who is a cookie freak — try searching your favorite cookies at eBay! I love snicker doodles (light, crisp cinnamon cookies) and found some at eBay by a blue-ribbon chef, *wsenterprises*. I checked the feedback and ordered (see Figure 13-3) some incredible cookies! The dee-lish cookies arrived in a day or so, and were packed beautifully — not one was broken. (The seller used air-popped popcorn in the box!) Think of these food items for birthday and special occasion gifts as well as for yourself!

Figure 13-3: Yummy, fresh cookies, baked to order.

If you travel and discover some regional or international food that you love, check eBay when you're back stateside. I came back from Jamaica and was hooked on Jamaican Blue Mountain Coffee. Much to my chagrin, this coffee retails for about $30 a pound! After a quick search, I found that I can easily purchase the same coffee at eBay for half that amount!

Finding food coupons

Do you go through the Sunday newspaper looking for coupons so that you can save on your weekly groceries? Of course you do — you love a bargain or you wouldn't be reading this book. Well, you're not alone — coupons are used every day to save money in the bricks-and-mortar grocery stores.

Wouldn't it be great to have as many coupons as you want for expensive items that you frequently use? See figure 13-4. A small number of knowledgeable eBay sellers buy multiple copies of local newspapers, cut out the original manufacturer's coupons, and put them up for sale on the site. Note that I used the search engine trick, by searching for *(coupon, coupons)*.

Show picture	Item Title	Price	Bids	Time Left
	All Categories 6507 items found for **(coupon,coupons)** Sort by items: **ending first** | newly listed | lowest priced | highest priced			Save this search
	40 Slim Fast Drink coupons-3.00/1 multipack	**$1.80**	4	1m
	40 Dawn (any size) coupons-.30/1	**$1.00**	1	2m
	35 free bowling coupons/gift certificates ⌂	**$10.99**	2	4m
	20 Coupons FREE Welch's Jam, Jelly or Spread	**$4.27**	11	4m
	20 Coupons Lipton Chailatta Chai Tea Mix	**$0.99**	-	4m
	$18.50 PAMPERS/BABY COUPONS. FREE SHIPPING	**$6.00**	10	4m
	40 Suave FREE Deodorant coupons with purchase	**$1.00**	1	5m
	Similac Formula Coupons/Checks $12	**$5.50**	3	5m

Figure 13-4: Over 6,000 sales for coupons — if you use 'em — here they are!

As Seen on TV

If you see a super kitchen item on TV (it slices, it dices, but wait, there's more), and you think you'd like to purchase it at a savings, run a search at eBay.

When you purchase from a seller at eBay — you may not only be saving money, you'll be protected by eBay's fraud protection program. Something you're not likely to have when you call a 1-800 number you see in an ad at 2:00 a.m. on TV.

I just ran a search for *popeil* (Ron Popeil is the self-appointed king of stuff nobody needs, and the inventor of the Pocket Fisherman, Ronco PastaMaker, the Showtime Rotisserie, Hair-in-a-Can, and hundreds more "must-have" items) at eBay and discovered two things:

  ✔ **Some eBay sellers can't spell:** I found 81 items while searching for *popeil* and 8 while searching for *popiel*.

  ✔ **Misspellings aren't all bad:** Nobody was bidding on the misspelled items, and savvy shoppers can get some incredible deals.

A search for *ronco* (the name of the company he founded) netted another 121 items that never mentioned Popeil.

If you're looking for a new item that is currently being advertised through commercials and infomercials, add *TV* to your search phrase. That way you can weed out similar items that are made by different manufacturers. A search for *as seen on tv* currently returns 1,724 items. When looking for these items, beware of low Buy It Now prices — they usually go hand in hand with high shipping charges.

Finding Outdoor Supplies on the Cheap

Getting your summer happening is a cinch at eBay. You can always find great bargains on pool supplies, patio furniture, and (especially in the winter) patio heaters. When I've searched for such items at eBay, I've found prices that (even including shipping costs) can beat my prices at the local discount store.

Keeping your green thumb happy

You no longer have to find a special nursery to find rare and unique plants. Just read your landscaping book and run a search at eBay for the plants you want. You can find almost every exotic plant you desire. Here's a lay of the land:

- Horticulturists from the Pacific Northwest are selling seeds and flats of their cherished lavender and herbs.

- A nursery in Indiana, *rosemeadownursery,* specializes in miniature roses, and is selling them by the dozen for spring. I ordered five, and they arrived packed so carefully it was amazing.

- Sellers from Hawaii are selling cuttings and seeds from those luscious Hawaiian plants.

I have bought some unique plants at eBay, including a dwarf Cavendish banana, a dwarf pomegranate and a plumeria *(frangipani)* cutting from Hawaii. Last year, I grew Atlantic giant pumpkins (to the delight of the kids in the neighborhood at Halloween time) and now can find the seeds for this very special pumpkin at eBay this year!

The Green Dragon Chair Company

To me, few things are more comfortable than sitting outside on a spring day on one of those incredibly comfortable Adirondack chairs. You can find lots of those chairs at eBay, but the Green Dragon Chair Company (represented by seller, *jrousch00*) is special. It sells a pre-sanded, partially assembled pine chair kit. All you need to do is use simple hand tools to put the chair together, and when you're done you can paint or stain the chair according to your preference. The Green Dragon also gives you a lovely color coffee cup to commemorate your purchase.

Click on a picture to enlarge

The Green Dragon is the mascot for Lake Placid High School in Florida, and the chairs are the brainchild of instructor John Rousch to raise funds for the school shop program. Putting together the chair kits gives students the opportunity to use power tools and shop machines, use layout and design techniques, do shop math, learn craftsmanship, and develop teamwork.

Mr Rousch teaches more than woodcraft production; the students get a taste for marketing, distribution, price points, and everything else you can think of that is associated with running a business. Mr. Rousch doesn't believe in working his students without rewarding them, either. Every time the kids sell 50 chairs, he throws a pizza party.

There are rules for nurseries that ship to different states. Some states require bare root shipping. The seller removes all dirt from the plant roots and ships the plant in a moisture-laden container. California, Washington, Oregon, Nevada, Utah and Arizona have special plant rules. More information can be found on the eBay help page: http://pages.ebay.com/help/policies/plantsand seeds.html.

Or click Site Map on the Navigation Bar. On the site map, look for an Is My Item Allowed at eBay? and click it.

Swimming pool equipment

Yes, eBay has its share of 6-foot inflatable alligators, water wings, underwater exercisers, and swimming-pool basketball sets. But eBay is also an excellent place to save money on swimming pool equipment and parts.

Anyone who has ever used a mechanical pool sweep knows that they are pretty temperamental items, and you need to work on them from time to time. There are sellers at eBay who sell brand new replacement parts for these pool monsters at a major savings from your local pool store.

Pool equipment of all kinds, including test equipment and supplies, can be found at lower-than-discount prices.

Calling all sports

One of the best aspects of getting involved in a sport is buying all the stuff you need to perform the sport looking your best. You can, of course, find individual sellers devoted to all your sporting needs, but eBay also has complete stores devoted to sports, as well. eBay covers everything you need, whether you are a participant or merely a fan. You won't find better bargains anywhere.

You can look for everything from camping equipment, to paintball supplies, and even curling. (Yes, curling.) When it comes to golf, I know that my lousy game isn't half as lousy when I look good, and I can find lots of things that I need at eBay.

 You may want to rent (or buy) a timeshare for your vacation. If you want to practice your game, you might want books and videos or get practice nets and putting greens for your home or office. See how a theme is put together? You also might want golf memorabilia (a Tiger Woods 1996 Rookie card, PSA 10, is worth $37,000), autographs, perhaps even a pair of tickets to the Ryder Cup or the Masters.

Themes can be a very valuable way to get what you want at eBay. See how we use themes in Chapter 12 to put together a wedding!

I was totally blown away when I saw pool tables for sale at eBay! *zBilliards* has been selling full-size billiard tables at eBay for a few years. He originally got interested in using eBay in his business when he saw his mother's collectible business turn from pretty good to a pretty big money maker with a little help from eBay.

Shopping themes for golf

eBay goes the distance to use related items to put together *themes.* The categories can get fairly narrow. But themes are put together with items from many categories with a related theme. Like when you're looking for things for golf, many things go into that theme. Find the eBay Golf theme page at http://pages.ebay.com/promo/golf. On this page, eBay gives close to a hundred links related to the world of golf.

You can buy golf clubs (like woods, irons, and putters), balls, and other equipment (like bags, carts, stands, umbrellas, and divot tools). You can also buy clothing to wear while you play golf (gloves, shirts, and shoes), and you can bid to book tee times at golf courses around the country.

Adam Ginsberg is the man behind *zBilliards.* (Check out one of his auctions in Figure 13-5.) He contracted directly with overseas factories to produce the tables according to his own exacting specifications (talk about branding!). He imports the tables directly and keeps them in his Los Angeles warehouse.

I've seen tables sell at eBay for as low as $710, and a quick glance at the feedback rating tells me that Ginsberg has plenty of happy customers. Many of the feedbacks also reflect comments by the installers that the tables bought from Ginsberg were half (or even one-third) the local purchase price.

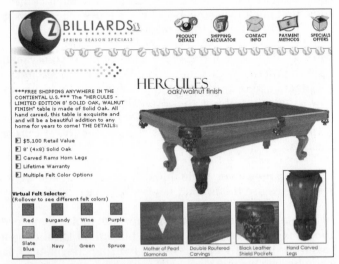

Figure 13-5: An auction from *zBilliards* begins at $1, and many tables sell with no reserve.

Holiday Fun and Decor

It doesn't take a whole lot of creative thinking to realize that eBay has to be the home for tons of ultra-cool holiday chic. Where else do you think you can find old-fashioned electric revolving color wheels for sale? There's quite a market for early-1960s aluminum Christmas trees! The eBay venue is one of the few places where you can actually have your pick of 6-foot pom-pom aluminum trees!

There may be a great market for ornaments and holiday collectibles, but what about the more common decorations, like wreaths and trees. Yes, Virginia, you can buy your Christmas tree at eBay (see Figure 13-6).

Finally, Christmas tree farmers have a venue of their own. No longer do they have to hack down their best trees and sell them to wholesalers that truck the trees across the country. Farmers are keeping their Grade #1 trees (according to National Christmas Tree Association standards) and selling them at eBay. Your tree will be hand-picked and babied all year, and cut just for you when you place your order at eBay.

Figure 13-6: Looking for a six-and-a-half foot blue spruce for $39.95, plus shipping (shipping $25)? Check out auctions from *jbeffel*.

My Christmas tree is coming from eBay from now on. I'm tired of walking through lots and seeing trees that are already semi-crispy. I want a fresh tree and wreath straight from the farm!

Chapter 14

Finding Digital and Industrial Bargains

· ·

· ·

*O*ne of the first things sold at eBay was founder Pierre Omidyar's broken down laser pointer. I guess that qualifies as the first "electronic" item sold on the site. Today electronics — for home and business use — are some of the most popular items on the site. Here's a chapter about everything you knew you could get at eBay — I'm sure that you had no idea how much there really is.

I can't possibly go through every interesting type of item sold in this category, so go visit the Electronics hub page (see Figure 14-1). You can get there from the link on the eBay home page or go directly to `http://pages.ebay.com/catindex/catelectronics.html`) where eBay has links to all the varied electronics subcategories.

You will also find loads of factory-refurbished items here among the new and used. For more information on refurbished items, check out Chapter 17.

Figure 14-1: The eBay Electronics hub.

Finding Home Electronics at eBay

Home electronics encompasses a wide amount of merchandise that eBay puts in the category of Electronics and Computers. The subcategories in Electronics and Computers are varied, and they include many of my favorites.

An important caveat here: If you're not familiar with certain brands or technologies, I suggest you study up before you jump in to shop for higher-end electronics such as computers and peripherals. Know what you want, know what options are important to you, and know what you want to do with the electronics you're thinking about bidding on. Here are some additional tips to keep in mind:

- ✔ Check current street prices at www.dealtime.com.
- ✔ Get reviews on how other people judged the items you're looking at from www.epinions.com.
- ✔ Read reviews from the pros at www.beststuff.com (see Figure 14-2).

If you're anything like me, this category covers the gear you use, and always want to upgrade. eBay sellers sell these items at such a

Figure 14-2: BestStuff.com reviews everything from the latest electronics to toys.

discount that you can afford an extra serving of the special niceties of life! Heck, you're not alone — $10 million a day gets spent on electronics alone at eBay. Below are some of the main subcategories of merchandise in this category.

PDAs

PDA stands for *personal digital assistant*. These devices are the ever-popular Palms and Windows Pocket PC devices. But wait, there's more: eBay is loaded with (currently over 25,000) the latest and greatest PDAs, with auctions for Compaq iPaq, Sony Clie, Hewlett Packard Jornada, and more.

The best part about this category is that if you can't afford to be the absolutely cutting edge. If you can't get the top-of-the-line, latest designs, you can get super deals on last year's technology. (Last year's technology is just fine with me!)

I got my PDA at eBay and I got my daughter's last two PDAs at eBay. (My husband still has an address book and is proud of it!) We got all the accessories we needed; extra styli, cleaners, and even a keyboard. I purchased elegant leather Dooney & Burke (very high-style) cases for the Palm PDAs for under $10 each.

Phones and wireless devices

You're no longer at the mercy of your cellular company when it comes to buying accessories for your phones. At eBay the items are a good deal cheaper than the mall kiosks and retailers. You can afford to get all the chargers and faceplates you want for your phones at lower-than-low prices.

Portable audio

Here you will find the newest items, and many that are factory refurbished. This is a great category to go to for holiday gifts as the savings are amazing here, especially in the new MP3 players!

Computers and Office Gear

When it comes to computers and computer accessories — eBay is number one. New and used units can be found at low, low discount prices. The big computer stores may be able to buy at lower prices, but they pay a higher overhead, so the discounts rarely get passed down to consumers. (Even though a few of the name-brand computer companies have their own stores at eBay.)

There are top-of-the-line computers at eBay (sold by sellers with excellent feedback) for hundreds of dollars less than retail stores. Many include warranties and provide telephone tech support from the manufacturer.

Even if you don't get your computers here, you'd be foolish not to get your ink cartridges and computer accessories here. Small businesses are doing land office business at eBay selling inkjet and laser printer consumables and specialty papers. You just can't find these items anywhere else at these prices! Check out the deal in Figure 14-3. This is a high-quality printer that's been refurbished (and includes a warranty) and could run a small business for years!

Here's a list of other home computing supplies you can find great deals on:

✓ **Blank CDs:** I'll bet you need blank CDs for backing up your files and for making musical compilations for, um, *personal* use. Match the prices you find at eBay with the local super-store, and you'll be having them delivered to your door.

✔ **Software:** New software comes out, and the prices seem to get more expensive every year. Stock of old versions of the software may end up with the liquidators — and liquidators can unload perfectly good, unregistered software at eBay for a fraction of the price you'd pay for new programs.

Older software versions may not have all the bells and whistles of the new software, but it may just handle what you need.

See more of what eBay has for business later in this chapter.

Home audio, video, and photo equipment

In addition to small sellers, you'll find many major retailers selling their excess inventory here. You'll find home theater systems, VCRs, DVDs, and everything else you need and never have to leave home again.

If you know where to look, the bargains in this area can be significant; a friend of mine just bought an outdated Bose home theater sound system for a fraction of the original retail price. Kind of like a Rolls Royce, the old Bose is better than many of the new, less-expensive systems that are for sale nowadays!

Figure 14-3: This Hewlett Packard printer sold from *Prefixtech* at eBay for only $305!

Be protected with an eBay warranty

If you worry about buying electronics at eBay — don't! You can purchase a warranty for almost any new, used, or refurbished electronic product you buy for personal use. (If the product is used or refurbished, it must be less than 5 years old.)

The warranty is supplied by the NEW (National Electronics Warranty Corporation) Service group exclusively through eBay and covers

✔ One year of product protection

✔ 100 percent coverage on parts and labor costs (and no deductible)

✔ 24/7 toll-free customer service

✔ "No Lemon" coverage — if the item requires more than three repairs, it's replaced

✔ Protection against power surges

You can extend a manufacturer's warranty that comes with a new product or buy a warranty for an item you buy. The warranty begins 30 days after the end date of the sale. Offers like this usually sound too good to be true, but this one isn't. The cost of the warranty is very reasonable and is based on what you pay for the item. For example, you can extend the warranty on a $4,000 plasma TV for only $299.99. For more details, visit `http://pages.ebay.com/help/warranty/buyer_overview.html`.

You can also get some sweet deals on digital still and digital video cameras. You can always find new and refurbished merchandise from business sellers, of course. But you can also find auctions for used (and perfectly good) cameras from people who are upgrading to new technology. If you don't mind staying one step behind, you can get some great deals!

Recorded Home Entertainment

If having a library of all the great movies is your goal, eBay is the place to go, and buying used can offer amazing savings. In Chapter 13, I told you about buying textbooks from the eBay-owned Half.com. You can do the same with CDs, DVDs and videos. At Half.com, just search for your media by title or keywords.

To find the listings at eBay, click <u>Movies & DVDs</u> in the category list on the eBay home page, or go to `http://pages.ebay.com/catindex/movies.html`.

Don't assume all you are going to find here are used disks — you'll find brand new, shrink wrapped disks and videos at low prices — and the selection is better than at most stores.

If you're looking for family-oriented videos, you can snap up libraries of discontinued videos from parents whose children have outgrown them!

Buying Goods for Business

Aside from all the bargains you can find in the computer and software areas, there's an amazing wealth of business products at eBay. eBay "officially" opened its business area in January 2003, but savvy business buyers have successfully used the site as a venue for this type of transaction for years.

The category started small and grew under eBay's radar, reaching today's 500,000 listings a week. Now you can not only get there from eBay's home page, but it has its own address:

`http://pages.ebay.com/catindex/business.html`

You'll find the "official" eBay Business hub at `www.ebay business.com` (see Figure 14-4).

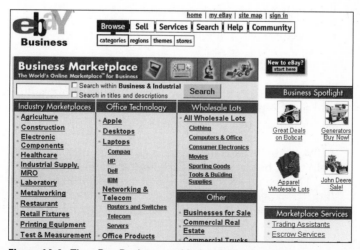

Figure 14-4: The eBay Business and Industrial home page.

TIP

If you think that the cost of shipping furniture will negate any savings you might get from buying at eBay, think again. The wildly popular Aeron chair by Herman Miller is often sold at eBay. You can buy it new for about a third of its retail value (and that includes shipping); you can buy a used Aeron chair for even less.

Here's a list of typical items I found when I took a look:

✔ A two-ton "12 SEER" (whatever *that* means) brand-name air conditioner sold for $202.50 (repossessed, never used)

✔ A pallet of 27,000 #000 Bubble Mailers from the eBay store, *GraMur Supply Co* (those had a nice Buy It Now price of $2,686.90)

✔ A new, royal 600SC cash register with a bar code scanner — what a bargain at $225

✔ A 6-foot-long refrigerated deli display case sold for $499

Finding Goods by Industry

The eBay community has established true vertical industry marketplaces. Don't believe me? Examine the site, and you will see equipment and supplies for the following industries:

✔ Construction

✔ Medical

✔ Commercial printing

✔ Restaurant and food service

✔ Test and measurement

I think you get the picture. . . .

My point? Sellers at eBay are filling the needs of traditional bricks-and-mortar businesses. eBay has come full circle from a personal shopping site to a professional supply site.

I have many friends in varied lines of commerce who ask me to help them buy very specialized items that are used in their industry. This isn't a PR spin. It's a real movement in fulfillment for industrial needs. Take a look at some of the eBay stores that sell industrial goods. See Figure 14-5 for the Reliable Tools store.

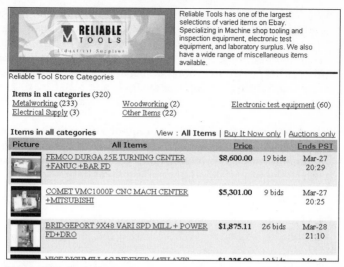

Figure 14-5: Find this store at `www.stores.ebay.com/ reliabletoolstore`.

How eBay buyers get lower prices

Early in 2000, I took a bet that I couldn't sell a concrete pump at eBay. For those of you who aren't familiar with this piece of equipment, it is the gizmo that concrete goes through when it comes out of that big truck and goes into the hose. Concrete pumps are expensive items, and I would assume it's fairly expensive to keep them in stock.

I went to the manufacturer's representative and found out how much the pumps usually sell for. I asked the rep if he could help me estimate shipping costs, and he said fine. I had to list the concrete pump twice (the first time it didn't sell), but with the second listing it sold. Best of all, the buyer lived near the factory and also saved by picking up the pump!

Realize that any seller can do this — be it selling cars, concrete pumps, or computers. Much of the expense that retailers bear in selling high-ticket items is in keeping the merchandise around (and waiting to recoup their money). Many eBay sellers sell items in this very same manner. The manufacturer gets the price and because the seller has very little overhead, he or she can be happier with a lower profit percentage than a retailer that sells the items.

By the way, the winner paid $4,000 below retail, and I made a cool $1,500 for my efforts.

When the eBay business site was launched, eBay let me know about a machine shop in Gainesville, Georgia. The shop, called DDTI, was a small business that got the bulk of its start-up equipment at eBay. DDTI's president purchased welders, drill presses, laboratory equipment, sensors, electrical enclosure valves and fittings, computer systems and a 10-ton, roof-mounted air conditioner.

The burgeoning business owner spent $100,000 on equipment for his business startup — a saving of approximately $750,000 off of manufacturers' list prices. What a great way to begin a business with top equipment and not ending up in debt.

Part V
Specialty Shopping

The 5th Wave   By Rich Tennant

"Oh, that there's just something I picked up as a grab bag
special from the 'Everything Else' category."

In this part. . .

The great thing about eBay is that it lets you shop for
whatever you want, whenever you want, and however
you want. No other auction venue offers the versatility of
specialty sites like Half.com and Sotheby's.com, the
immense selection of eBay stores (which allow sellers to
sell items in a more traditional online retail format), the
convenience of shopping regionally, and the value of shopping for closeouts. The chapters here show you what you
need to know to shop smart while exploring eBay's nooks
and crannies.

Chapter 15

Getting Particular with Specialty Sites

*E*ven though each and every one of eBay's categories (and themes as well) is its own *specialty site,* eBay runs a few bona fide specialty sites — that is, sites that are actually *separate.* You can miss a bunch of great deals if you ignore these side sites of eBay.

Half.com is a very successful specialty site of eBay. You can purchase anything and everything there, but it does a great job for buying media: books, CDs, DVDs and videos. It will become part of the eBay site in 2004. Learn more about shopping there in Chapter 13.

eBay's site search may not reveal all the bargains listed in these nooks 'n' crannies, so read on and get the goodies.

Shopping eBay Stores

eBay stores are the secret weapon for knowledgeable eBay shoppers. First, of course, you can consistently find great deals. But you can also help small businesses make it against larger behemoths. Sellers open eBay stores to make searching merchandise easier for buyers; stores also help save sellers money because sellers don't need to set up private e-commerce Web sites. Translation? Sellers can list items in their eBay stores for even lower fees, thereby passing their savings on to you, the savvy bargain hunter.

TIP

Before you buy any item from a sale at eBay, check to see if the seller has the small, red *stores* icon next to his or her User ID. If so, be sure to click the icon *before* you bid on the item. Most sellers run auctions for items to draw people into their eBay stores, where you may be able to purchase the exact same item you're about to bid on — for a lower amount.

You can find the eBay Stores hub from the eBay home page by clicking the eBay Stores link under the Specialty Sites heading. You can also get there by typing in the Web address, www.ebay stores.com. The eBay Stores hub is shown in Figure 15-1.

On the eBay Stores hub you'll see a small group of six store logos in the center of the page. These store logos change every few minutes as eBay rotates its *anchor stores* through the area. Store owners pay a considerable amount to have their stores listed as anchor stores. (If you're unfamiliar with the anchor store concept, think of it as the high-rent district of eBay stores. When you go to the mall, the big department stores like Macy's or Bloomingdale's are the anchor stores.)

Below the store logos is a list of clickable links to stores. These are *featured stores.* You guessed it; this place has a higher real estate value than a regular eBay store.

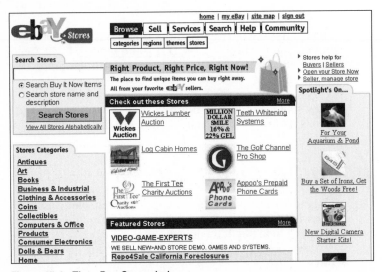

Figure 15-1: The eBay Stores hub.

You can find more stores, including the smallest ones — the cottage industry sellers — by clicking one of the stores' categories links on the left side of the page.

Searching the stores

eBay stores cannot be searched through the same search engine you use to search for eBay auction items, but that doesn't mean your search options are limited. In fact, you can find your items in eBay stores through several methods. One way is by clicking the Sales icon next to a seller's User ID. The following sections offer you a couple more search options.

A clue in regular eBay Search

When you run a regular search for an item at eBay, you'll see a column of yellow boxes of links on the left side of the results page. If you scroll down to the bottom of the More at eBay area, you see links to eBay stores that may carry the item you are looking for, as shown in Figure 15-2.

Figure 15-2: Look for this heading to find related stores when you do a typical search for auction items.

The links that are listed may not show *all* the stores that carry your item, but if you're lucky, they'll get you started.

Searching through eBay's Search page

When you click the box in eBay's Navigation Bar that takes you to the Search area, you see a Search Stores tab. Click this tab to visit the Search Stores page (see Figure 15-3).

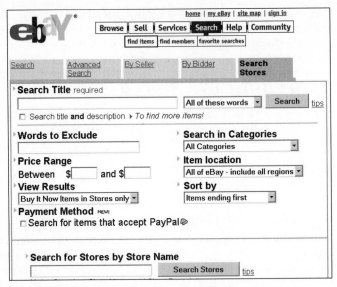

Figure 15-3: Searching stores from the eBay Search page.

If you want details on how each of the search modifiers on this page work, take a look at Chapter 10. Just remember that when you search stores from the Search Stores tab of the eBay search, you'll be searching stores alone. You must search eBay separately from the Advanced Search or the Search tab of this area.

On the Search Stores tab, you can search stores in the exact area you would perform the auction search, from the Search tab. Also added is the option (in case you remember all or part of a seller's store name) is a Search for Stores by Store Name box. (This option also lets you search the store description.) Just type as much as you can remember of the store name (in the case of my store, just enter my last name, **collier** and a word from my store description, **dummies**), click Search Stores, and you'll be presented with a list of store names that match your search.

Searching from the eBay Stores hub page

If you look back at Figure 15-1, you'll see a Search Stores box on the left-hand side of the page. You have a couple of options when you search from this page:

✔ **Click in the Search Buy It Now Items box:** The search engine goes through all the items listed in all the eBay stores to find your selected keywords in the item title. (Searching eBay stores from the eBay search page allows you to search both item titles and item descriptions in stores.)

✔ **Click the Search Store Name and Description button:** The store search engine will search only the store names, and the brief store description posted by the seller.

Browsing eBay stores

Looking back on Figure 15-1, below the search box, you'll see a category listing that's similar to the one on the eBay home page. The only difference is that when you click these categories, you're browsing eBay stores by category — and not the rest of the eBay auction categories. Each category has a home page very similar to the Stores hub page (see Figure 15-4).

The main category of the eBay Stores page shown in Figure 15-4 is Clothing & Accessories. When you look at the left side of this page, you can view the store's subcategories.

When you click a subcategory (such as Women) you are able to view the subcategory pages. Figure 15-5 shows the Women subcategory of the Clothing & Accessories category.

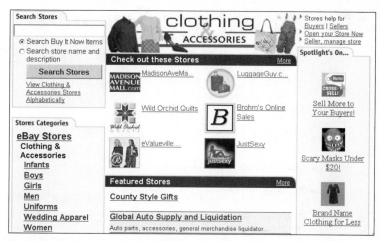

Figure 15-4: The eBay Stores Clothing & Accessories category.

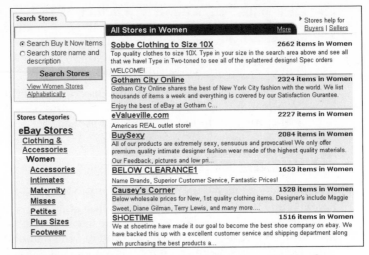

Figure 15-5: The Women subcategory of eBay Stores Clothing & Accessories.

You'll note that on the left side, even more subcategories are listed. Right down the center of the page is a listing of all stores in the Women subcategory. The stores are listed in descending order; the stores with the most items are at the top of the list, and the stores with the fewest are at the end.

Checking Out an eBay Store

When you finally arrive at the eBay store of your choice, you'll see a page that looks similar to the one in Figure 15-6. An eBay store not only lists the items that the seller has listed in the store, but also every active auction or Buy It Now item the seller has placed on the eBay site.

All eBay stores have four clickable tabs:

- ✔ **Store items:** The home page of the store.
- ✔ **Feedback:** The seller's feedback.
- ✔ **Store policies:** The terms and conditions of the seller's auctions.
- ✔ **About the store:** The seller's About Me page (see Chapter 5 for more on About Me pages).

Figure 15-6: The home page of my eBay store.

You'll see several things on every eBay store home page:

- ✔ **eBay Stores logo:** Instead of the eBay logo in the upper-left corner, you'll see the eBay Stores logo. A click here brings you to the eBay stores home page.

- ✔ **eBay Navigation Bar:** I told you that you can't get rid of this; the eBay Navigation Bar also appears at the top of every eBay store page.

- ✔ **The store name:** The name the store owner has chosen for the store. The store name helps you remember the Web address. Each eBay store has its own address that ends in the eBay store's name, like this: www.stores.ebay.com/insert storename. For example, my store's URL is www.stores. ebay.com/marshacolliersfabulousfinds.com.

- ✔ **Seller's User ID and feedback rating:** Below the store name, next to Maintained by is the seller's User ID. And of course, the ubiquitous feedback rating.

- ✔ **Add to my Favorite Stores:** If you click this link, the store is added to your My eBay Favorites page on your My eBay area.

- ✔ **Search box:** To the right of the store name, is a search box that allows you to search all the items this seller has for sale.

- ✔ **Store logo and description:** In the middle of the page is the store's graphic logo, and to the right of that is the seller's description of the store. (This is the area that is searched when you search *Stores by Store Name and Description*.)

✔ **Store categories:** eBay store owners may assign their own custom categories to the items they sell to better organize things within the store. You may click on individual categories to see items in that classification for that seller.

eBay Live Auctions and Sothebys.com

When it comes to special items, this is the place to go. From the eBay home page, take a look at the links on the right. At the very top of the column of links is a link to Sothebys.com. At the very bottom of the category link is a link to Live Auctions.

Ladies, you don't have to put on diamond jewelry and get all dressed up to attend these auctions. And gentlemen, black tie is not necessary. As a matter of fact, you can now bid against the Vanderbilts from your home in your jammies and fuzzy slippers. Champagne and caviar hors d'oeuvres are optional.

In these areas, you and I can bid on the most high-profile auctions from around the world at the world's most famous auction houses.

If you don't want to bid, you can use the viewing function where you can watch the bidding on your screen in real time with the auction house floor, by indicating (during or just before the live auction) on the site that you'd like to just watch the action. All the software is in your browser — you need nothing special.

When you bid in live auctions, whether on Sothebys.com or at eBay Live Auctions, you will no doubt be required to pay a *buyer's premium*. A buyer's premium is an amount, added to the winner's final bid, which goes to the auction house. The premium usually runs between 15 and 20 percent of the final sale price. Before you sign up for the auction, be sure to read all the terms and conditions of the auctioneer and factor this extra charge into your highest bidding price before you even consider placing a bid.

When you come to the home page of the individual live auctions, be sure to click the link to <u>View All Lots</u>. That way you can see all of the items up for sale in the individual auctions. That's how you'll find the unseen gem.

You don't have to be at your computer at the time of the auction to participate. You can place an absentee bid for the item on the auction page, and the bid is placed in your name by the auction house when the item comes up for bidding. Sometimes you may think you can't afford these great items, but many times items do go for low bids. You can't win if you don't play, so if you see something you really want bid. You just might win it.

eBay Live Auctions

The Live Auctions area of the eBay site is one of the most exciting places to visit, especially during an auction. If you look in this area, you'll have the opportunity to bid or watch an auction in live action (as shown in Figure 15-7) on some of the finest and most unique items in the world. I have personally spent many a fun afternoon with the smallest dream that I might be able to bid with the big boys on some of these special auctions.

Major auction houses from around the world run online auctions here at eBay, and every item up for sale is covered by traditional live auction guarantees. On the Live Auctions home page (http://pages.ebay.com/liveauctions) you can preview the upcoming sales to be held live on the site.

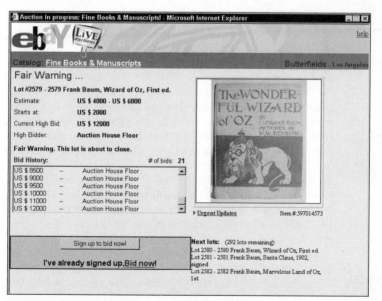

Figure 15-7: An auction that I thought I could afford, but alas . . . .

From this page, shown in Figure 15-8, you can view the entire catalog of items for sale in one of the upcoming live auctions. If you like the items in the auction, you can sign up to participate in the auction. You should do this in advance, just in case the auction house has to verify your credit card account information.

Figure 15-8: eBay Live Auctions home page.

Sothebys.com

Sotheby's is the world's oldest fine art auctioneer, and now it's making its mark at eBay. You can participate in any of Sotheby's many auctions run online through eBay. Live Sotheby's auctions from London and New York are also represented on the site, which can also be accessed directly at http://sothebys.ebay.com.

On the Sothebys.com home page (See figure 15-9), you can click categories by name (just like at eBay) and browse the various items that are coming up for sale. Just below the category searches are links to the upcoming auctions on the site.

Sotheby's recently made an alliance with eBay to run all its online auctions through eBay. The bricks-and-mortar auctioneer has sold some amazing items through its online auctions, like the record-setting first printing of the Declaration of Independence, which sold for a cool $8.14 million. Figure 15-10 shows a recent auction that I watched live on Sothebys.com.

Figure 15-9: Sothebys.com eBay home page.

Figure 15-10: A very special auction on Sothebys.com. (I couldn't afford this item either.)

Chapter 16

Shopping Close to Home

- -

In This Chapter

▶ Shopping regionally

▶ Shopping for large items

▶ Gifting for out-of-town friends

- -

I think by now you're probably convinced that eBay's a great place to shop for almost anything. Picture this: You're at home or at work, and suddenly you remember that the day after tomorrow is one of the following:

> a) Your boss's birthday
>
> b) Your sister-in-law's anniversary
>
> c) Your nephew's graduation

There isn't a moment in your schedule for an extended shopping trip, and you don't dare call your spouse because she pulled you out of the last disaster. eBay can come to the rescue — without exorbitant express shipping charges!

Even items that you wouldn't think you could buy at eBay because their size would cause prohibitive shipping charges (anyone looking for a piano?) are available at eBay. If you're worried about the shipping costs, don't be. eBay is one step ahead of you.

If you click on the Browse box on the eBay Navigation Bar, a drop-down sub-menu appears (see Figure 16-1). Click <u>Regions</u> for a pleasant surprise.

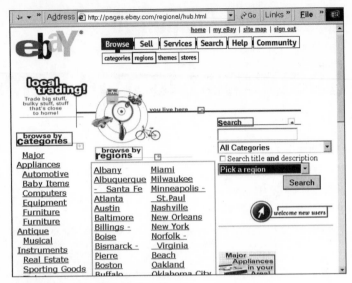

Figure 16-1: The eBay Regions page.

eBay's Local Trading Zones

Here's the place where eBay brings the world's marketplace closer to your hometown. The geography whizzes at eBay narrowed down the United States into 60 shopping regions. Whenever a seller posts an item at eBay, he or she is asked to indicate the regional trading area that's closest to home. This marks the auction for the eBay computers.

When you arrive at the local trading page, scroll down the page and find the metropolitan area closest to your home, it draws that piece of information from the item listing. Find the city of your choice and click it, and you'll find your own mini, local eBay!

Regional is just a means of displaying auction results.

Shopping for large items

The eBay Web site is not just the best place to look for small easily shippable items, but it's also great for bigger items. By shopping the region near your home, you'll be able to get some real bargains on large items that you'd probably never find any other way. No newspaper or penny-shopper can show you beautiful color pictures like you can see at eBay.

Recently there have been a group of sellers who sell large items like furniture — and even pool tables on the site — that offer shipping at no extra charge. Be sure to use the search term *free shipping* to see what kinds of results you come up with.

Home furnishings online

If you're looking for exquisite collectible antique furniture, this is the place. There's everything from Rococo to Chippendale to Eames, and I'll bet you can find something special close to your home.

You can find new furniture, too. In fact, I've seen furniture stores selling samples at eBay. You never know what will be up for sale on any given day.

You can find lots of lower-end and used furniture, too. Handy people can find vintage upholstered goods ready for refurbishing. Young people starting out can decorate an entire apartment or home right from eBay at bargain basement prices — and they can do their shopping together from their computer!

The average eBay auction lasts for seven days. You may not find just what you're looking for the moment you look for it. Check back once or twice a week to find your treasure. Better yet, set up a recurring search on your My eBay Favorites page, and arrange for eBay to e-mail you when it finds the item up for sale. For details on how to set this up, see Chapter 4.

Major appliances

One of the most amazing things that I've found at eBay is in the category of home appliances. As I'm writing, I just browsed through the category. If you want to get a gently used (but functioning) refrigerator, stove, washing machine, or dryer you have many to choose from. It's a perfect place to find items for people staring out.

For a collector, there was an absolutely immaculate 1950s Fridgidaire stove that looked like the one from the *I Love Lucy* TV series. I can just see Lucy serving Ricky a plate of eggs from it. It was selling for $175 to someone in Texas. I don't know what I would do with it, but it was sure beautiful. But, I digress . . .

Try conducting a search on top-quality, brand-name items like *Wolf, Sub-Zero, Gaggenau,* and *Viking.* You may discover that all these brands are available on the site, but maybe not in your area. Keep checking. You'll find new items, old items, all in various conditions ranging from slightly used to *very* used.

Finding Events, Tickets, and Experiences

I am very glad that I discovered the Tickets & Experiences area of eBay. I'm always the one who forgets to buy tickets to the hot play or concert in town until two weeks before it opens. Of course, by that time, the event is either sold out or the only seats available are single seats at different ends of the nose-bleed section. Once more, eBay saved my bacon.

Many people I know have a queasy feeling about buying tickets from someone who lists tickets for sale in the newspaper — are the tickets stolen? You have to meet these strangers somewhere, and they only want cash. Then there are always ticket brokers, who mark the price of their tickets up so high that they are unaffordable for the average person (that's me).

At eBay, regular people (with feedback ratings) in your area are selling tickets all the time. Some may have bought tickets way in advance and realize now that they're not able to go to the event. Others may have bought tickets for friends who didn't come up with the money. Or perhaps they may have stood in the line when the tickets went on sale to make a little profit; they're true eBay entrepreneurs.

If you go to the category list on the left side of eBay's home page and click the <u>Tickets</u> link, the Tickets hub appears, as shown in Figure 16-2. You can also go directly to `http://pages.ebay.com/catindex/ticketsexperience.html`.

On the Ticket Hub page, the first thing you'll find is the convenient Product Finder. It's a quick and easy way to find special events in your area. You can customize your search through drop-down boxes. Table 16-1 shows you the product finder selection options.

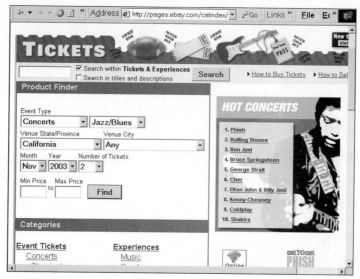

Figure 16-2: eBay's Events, Tickets & Experiences Hub page.

Table 16-1	Events, Tickets, and Experiences Categories
Category	*Subcategory*
Concerts	Any, Classical, Country, Jazz/Blues, Pop, R&B/Soul, Rap/Hip-Hop, Rock 'n' Roll, Other
Movies	No subcategory
Sporting Events	Any, Auto Racing, Baseball, Basketball-College, Basketball-Pro, Football-College, Football-Pro, Golf, Hockey, Soccer, Wrestling, Other
Theater	Any, Musicals, Plays, Other

Of course, you should select the state where you want to attend the event; doing so changes the drop-down box next to the state's name so that it contains the major cities (regions) in the state you chose. Select the city in which you would like to attend the event. Below, select the month, year, number of tickets and minimum and maximum ticket price (I suggest giving a wide range of prices here) you are looking for; click Find.

Gifting for out-of-town friends

Next to many items at eBay you may see a small gift box icon. The gift box icon means that the seller may gift wrap the item and ship it as a gift to another person and address. As you have learned, the seller isn't protected when they ship to an address other than your registered address, so sellers consider this a special concession to a buyer.

If you find an item that interests you as a gift, and the seller isn't showing the gift icon, don't be afraid to ask the seller (before you bid) if he or she would perform this service for you. Many a seller will respond positively to a nicely written note.

If you're just looking for a good time, you can leave out any of the specifications in your search. Let's say you have no idea what's going on in town — you'd just like to go out and do something. Just leave the event selection as *Any,* put in your city, month and year and see what pops up! Instant fun. Who knew Phish was in town?

Ticket sales are regulated by state laws. eBay follows the specific rules, so if you live in Arkansas, Connecticut, Florida, Illinois, Kentucky, Louisiana, Massachusetts, Michigan, Minnesota, New Mexico, New York, North Carolina, Pennsylvania, Rhode Island or South Carolina, you'll have to observe certain restrictions. To see all the legalese, go to `http://pages.ebay.com/help/community/png-tickets.html`.

Below the Product finder, you'll find the subcategories that also include Experiences. Experiences are often packages that include travel, or can be "one-of-a-kind" events. Some of the current one-of-a-kind items include hot air balloon rides, tours of old mines, and trips to go mining for gold. You can also find Disney travel packages, Iditarod race lodging, meals, and other activities. You get the idea. Experiences are unique.

Chapter 17

Shopping eBay's Bargain Basement

*O*ne of the reasons I originally gravitated toward eBay is that I dearly love getting a bargain. Getting merchandise of quality and saving money at the same time is right up there on my top ten list of favorite things to do.

I used to have the time to spend a day at an outlet mall and shop. But as life got busier, I would only go to outlet malls at sale time to get merchandise to sell at eBay. Now, alas, I don't even have time for that — but luckily, eBay has plenty of sellers who work just like the outlets you love in the bricks-and-mortar world. The trick is knowing how to find them!

Wandering Around eBay's Outlet Mall

I like to think of eBay's stores as a quick and easy outlet mall. Although I give you the straight scoop at eBay stores in Chapter 16, I'd like to give you a little close up of the types of retailers who have their outlets here at eBay. Search eBay's store names and descriptions from the main eBay Store page (see Figure 17-1) and you'll discover your favorite brands and stores.

To get to the search box shown in Figure 17-1, you have a choice. Go to www.ebaystores.com or click the <u>eBay Stores in the Specialty sites area</u> link on the eBay home page. When you get the eBay stores home page, the search box is in the upper-right corner, below the Navigation Bar.

Figure 17-1: Searching for brand-name outlets in eBay stores.

Major retailers who've set up shop here include Sears, Kodak, Samsonite, Sharper Image, Motorola, Ritz Camera, Dell, Amtrak (for selected routes), and more.

Do a search of eBay stores using words like *outlet* and *liquidation,* and you'll find some excellent buys.

Getting the Skinny on Refurbished Goods

You can find great deals on refurbished electronic merchandise at eBay. Unfortunately, refurbished merchandise gets an unnecessarily bad rap. Very smart people may tell you to be wary of refurbished merchandise. Great advice . . . I guess. I tell people to be wary of *all* merchandise.

The way I figure it, refurbished merchandised has been gone over by the manufacturer twice — new merchandise has only been gone over once! I buy refurbished merchandise all the time.

Let me explain what refurbished merchandise is, and why it can be such a bargain. Refurbished merchandise can fall into one of these categories:

✔ **Canceled orders:** This is merchandise that's in perfectly good shape. When a customer makes a special order and then changes his or her mind, or the order is somehow mucked up ("I ordered a PC. You sent me a Mac!"), something has to be done with the merchandise. Enter you, the savvy shopper.

✔ **Evaluation units:** An evaluation unit is a piece of equipment that is sent to a member of the media or to a corporation for testing or review purposes. Evaluation units must be returned to the manufacturer, and the manufacturer may decide to unload it for a couple of extra bucks.

✔ **Store returns:** This is probably pretty obvious to you, right? Joe Customer buys something in a store, takes it home, and opens it, only to decide that he doesn't really want it so much. By law, as soon as the box is opened, a piece of merchandise can never be sold as new again, even if the merchandise was never used.

✔ **Defective units:** A piece of merchandise that is deemed defective, either by the store or by the user, is returned to the manufacturer.

✔ **Overstocks:** When a manufacturer comes out with a new model, it may take back the older models from retailers in an effort to encourage them to stock more of the newer, faster, cooler model.

Whenever an item is returned to the manufacturer for any reason and the original box has been opened, the item (whether it is a television, a computer, a camera, or some other technical device), must be reconditioned to the manufacturer's original quality standards. Any parts that are non-functioning are replaced with functioning components, and the item is repackaged. The manufacturer usually gives refurbished items a 90-day warranty.

You can purchase an extended warranty that completely covers (yep, 100 percent) parts and labor on refurbished electronics you buy at eBay (with no deductibles). To find out more about eBay Warranty Services, check out Chapter 14. After your purchase, go to `http://smart.newcorp.com/ebay/jsp/EBAY-NewStep1.jsp`. You can also check out `http://pages.ebay.com/help/warranty/buyer_overview.html`.

Even after purchasing an extended warranty, the savings on refurbished name-brand merchandise can be substantial.

When buying refurbished goods, be sure the original manufacturer was the one doing the reconditioning. I'm sure that some technical geek can fix things just fine in his or her garage, but you don't have the same level of protection (as in, you don't have a warranty from a reliable source at all) if you buy a piece of equipment that wasn't fixed by the manufacturer.

Defining Liquidations

Liquidations could be about my favorite kind of bargain hunting. Merchandise can be new, used, or trashed. Searching through liquidators' auctions is like digging through the "Final Sale" bin at a store, where prices are marked down to absurd levels.

Liquidators buy merchandise from companies that are in financial distress and need to raise cash quickly. The kinds of issues companies face can vary — the why isn't important. All you need to know is that you can get access to some astonishing deals because some of it is sold piece by piece to the public at eBay.

Liquidators buy by the truckload (I'm talking 18-wheeler, not pickup). From there the merchandise is unloaded, inspected, and sorted — and then the fun begins. Some of the merchandise can be put together in wholesale *lots* (the goods are grouped together by the pallet or by the case and sold to wholesalers or retailers), and some of the merchandise may be put aside to be sold one by one to individual buyers at eBay.

Buying items from liquidators can be a risky enterprise. There's no warranty, and no one you can complain to if something is wrong with the item. All items are always sold *as is* and *where is*.

Essentially, what you see is what you get, if it works, it's a bonus.

Here are some tips for buying this type of item:

- **Look for a sealed box:** Look at the picture and read the description carefully. If it is stated that the item is sealed in the manufacturer's packaging, you've got a pretty good chance that the item is in new condition.

- **Don't spend a bundle:** This kind of goes without saying, right? It's supposed to be a bargain. Don't go crazy.

One of my favorite liquidators at eBay sells under two names, Bargainland-Media for DVDs and videos and Bargainland-Liquidation for literally everything else. This liquidator operates out of a 100,000-square-foot facility in Phoenix, and it has hundreds of loyal customers at eBay.

Bargainland does take hits with negative feedback as well. People are often unhappy when their dice shoot turns up snake eyes. I've bought from this liquidator as well, and have carefully steered clear of anything that wasn't a fairly safe bet. I also follow my own advice and rarely buy an item from Bargainland that isn't new in the manufacturer's box — or cheap enough to gamble with.

Table 17-1 shows a very short list of a few typical liquidation auctions and their final bids.

Table 17-1 Liquidation Auctions and Final Bids	
Auction Item	*Final Bid*
New Master Swing Personal Golf Driving Range	$8.02
New FitSense Speedometer FS-1 Watch $249	$77
$29 Deluxe Slimline Phone Caller ID	$1.54
New IBM Scroll Point III USB Black Mouse	$1
NEW $79 Bermuda Sands Mens 10 Golf Shoes	$5.05
New $149 AB-DOer Abdominal Workout	$33.58
NEW Fisher Price Safe Embrace Infant Car Seat	$17.50
American Tourister Teal Tapestry Boarding Bag	$12.05
$67 Outdoor Bronze Lighting Spotlight	$26
Women's Wilsons Pelle Studio Leather Jacket	$30
New Wild Rabbit Duck Ceramic Vase	$2.02
DKNY Black /White Hand Knit Size P Sweater	$5.25

Looks like fun doesn't it? But remember, there's always a risk. On *Bargainland-Liquidation's* About Me page, the company's policy is clearly stated. A portion of which is below:

We are not able to compensate customers for any discrepancies in product. We will, however, assure customers that they will get the EXACT merchandise that they see in the photo regardless of the description. Please keep in mind that liquidation is not for everyone.

Bargainland does not offer any refunds, warranties or returns of any kind for any reason. The only reason you will ever be given a refund by our company is if you did not receive the product shown in the photograph. Please consider this carefully before you buy.

Buyer beware — but have lots of fun!

Part VI
Going for the Gold

I didn't even know they sold sea monkeys on eBay, let alone ones that were used in tests done in outer space.

In this part. . .

*W*ant a car? A plot of land? A time share in Miami? An engagement ring? Look no further than Part VI. These chapters are a great help when looking for big-ticket items. I bought a time share on the ocean in Miami Beach at eBay, and my neighbor bought a car at eBay. We're both happy with our purchases and we saved big-time cash by shopping at eBay. Of course, shopping for the more expensive items can be a little scary. I tell you what you need to know to get your questions answered before you bid.

Chapter 18

Driving a Deal at eBay Motors

* *

* *

*I*f there's one purchase that I don't enjoy making it's buying a car. Please don't misunderstand. I love cars, and I have a personal attachment to every car I've ever owned. It's just that each time I'm approached by a car salesman, I get intimidated. The minute the salesman says, "I've got to check with my sales manager to see if I can do that," I just know I'm a goner.

And when I've finally decided on the car model I want, I still have to face *the deal,* when Mr. Sales Guy calls in the finance manager to try to sell me warranties, alarms, ups, and extras that I never wanted or needed. I guess I'm not a good car buyer. I feel the need to run out of the dealership — and I usually do.

If this feeling is familiar to you, I would like to introduce my fellow car buyers to the sweetest deal of the 21st century, eBay Motors. In 2003, eBay projects sales of over $2 billion in the eBay Motors venue alone. I'd say that makes eBay the largest auto mall in the universe.

On the down-to-earth side, Jupiter Media Metrix, the premier analyst of the Internet, recently ranked eBay Motors (shown in Figure 18-1) the number one automotive site on the Web.

Figure 18-1: The eBay Motors home page.

Introducing Motors

For some of us, eBay Motors is a magnificent fantasy site. I have a friend who browses the Volkswagen Bus category; his eyes glaze over with hope and awe as he reads each listing. I'm sure he's reliving his hippy days of the late '60s. Another friend reads the Ferrari and Lamborghini listings, he knows every color combination and variation; he pooh-poohs all the aftermarket changes to the classics. My best friend checks out the vintage Thunderbirds and pictures herself as Suzanne Sommers flirting with the guys in *American Graffiti*. Then of course there's my fantasy car; the buttercup yellow Rolls Royce Corniche driven by Teensy in *The Divine Secrets of the Ya-Ya Sisterhood*. (I've yet to find one at eBay in that color combination — but then again, I couldn't afford one if I did find it!)

I've known several people who have successfully purchased cars at eBay Motors. They couldn't have found deals like these at their home dealerships and are very, very happy with their purchases.

Many of the cars at eBay Motors are private party sales, bank cars (repossessions), and cars that have been cherry-picked by wholesalers and dealer overstocks. There are also the professional car dealers selling their rare, hard-to-find cars to a marketplace that draws between 4 to 5 million visitors per month. You can't get that many people through the door at a local dealership! Dealers put up the rare colors and limited-edition vehicles because this *is* an auction site, and the rarer an item the more likely bidders are to get excited. The more excited bidders are, the more they lose their heads — and the higher the price goes.

Yes, this is an auction, and the bidding goes hot and heavy, an average of seven to eight bids per auction. It's a very competitive environment for the most desirable cars. Dealers can sell cars for less at eBay, because it costs them less to sell. (They don't have to pay the finance manager to twist your arm to buy the ups and extras.) Cars sell quickly at eBay, and they're making money on volume, not by picking your pockets.

Enter the eBay Motors site in two ways, go to `www.ebaymotors.com` or click the <u>eBay Motors</u> link in the top-left corner of the eBay home page.

Finding More Than Cars

The truly amazing part about eBay Motors is that it has more than just the usual cars and vans. In fact, the rule seems to be that if it has an engine, you'll find it right here. You can find just about anything to get you from one place to another. Here's a description of the *Other Vehicles* categories:

- ✔ **ATVs:** Within the ATV category you'll find a wide selection of new and used 4-x-4s and 2-x-4s; You can find 3 wheelers and 4 wheelers. I even found a few six-wheel amphibious vehicle! Bidding in this category is very active, and the items move quickly.

- ✔ **Aircraft:** Anything that flies can be found here: hot air balloons to military trainer jets. Browsing this category is amazing, who could imagine that with a click of your mouse (and enough money), you could own your own Bell helicopter or Gulfstream jet. If you've ever even dreamt of taking up flying, this just might be the category to get your hobby started!

- ✔ **Boats & Watercraft:** This category was so full that I got seasick just browsing! It has its own subcategories of Fishing Boats, Personal Watercraft (Sea-Doo, Yamaha, Kawasaki, and so on.), Powerboats, Sailboats, and others (kayaks, canoes, pontoons, tenders and dinghies). I know boats, and I saw some incredible deals in this category. There were some beautiful Bass boats and Boston Whalers at incredible prices. There were also a dozen or so Bayliners that caught my eye, especially the 47-foot Pilot House Motoryacht with a starting bid of $290,000 *(sigh)*. It was also nice to see a wide selection (pricewise) for sailboats. With some time spent shopping in the category, you can find just about anything you want; within your price range.

✔ **Buses, Motorcoaches:** No kidding. You want to start your own bus line? Here's the place to find the busses — and it seems that plenty of people are interested in them! There's active bidding on old school busses and coaches in this category (and I thought the American family was getting smaller).

✔ **Commercial Trucks:** Since commercial trucks are something I know jack about, I went to some experts who browsed the site and examined the deals. Here's their review for those in the know. The items are good quality, and the type they'd like to find at good commercial truck auctions. The prices are good bargains, and they say they will be visiting the site regularly from now on — sounds like a good recommendation to me!

✔ **Scooters & Minibikes:** Aside from what you'd expect to find here, this is the home for beautiful vintage and new Vespa motor scooters.

✔ **Snowmobiles:** Since I've never really lived in a snow part of the country, I can only imagine how much fun these bad boys are! The bidding for snowmobiles is very active, right now averaging 15 bids each! Again, you'll see everything from top-of-the-line new ones to gently used, private party sales.

✔ **Miscellaneous:** Now this is some great stuff! How about a 1947 Coca-Cola vending truck — complete with fountain, cotton candy machine and propane-powered hot dog cooker! Sounds like a carnival on wheels! Well, okay, it doesn't run, buy hey — it's only $3,000! There's also a Shelby Cobra kit, no motor or tranny — but you need a hobby, don't you? I also found a Think Neighbor electric vehicle; a sandrail dunebuggy four-seater; go-carts and car haulers. There's nothing you can't find at eBay!

Getting the Deals

Depends what you call a deal. If you consider it a deal to even have the opportunity to buy the 2003 Ford Thunderbird Limited Edition (only 700 made), James Bond 007 Roadster for $45,995 — hey — this is the place to find the deals! If that's not enough room, there's also a 1999 Bentley Continental SC (only 1 of 14) with a Targa top; Buy It Now for only $220,000!

Collectors can find the best of the best at eBay. You're not limited to the lag time of a published magazine or by what's available when you're at a dealership. You've got the world at your fingertips (or at your mouse-clicks). Now, for the rest of us. Sigh. When I was growing up, I heard the words "reliable transportation" quite a bit when it came to buying a car. When I was in college, reliable transportation was important, but it faded just a bit; the "cool factor" slid into first place on my list of what was important when buying a car.

eBay Motors offers thousands of good reliable cars every day on the site — some of them are loaded with cool.

Finding your dream car

eBay Motors is laid out in a very matter-of-fact, organized manner. From the home page, click <u>Cars</u>, to see another page of subcategories that lists about every car manufacturer you have ever heard of, and even one or two you probably haven't thought of in a while (like DeLorean and Avanti).

If you don't have a particular car in mind; you might at least have a manufacturer you're interested in. You can just click the name and browse the category.

How much cash should you spend?

Of course budget is a personal thing. But there are a couple of sites on the Internet that can give you a very good idea of what you should expect to spend on a new or used vehicle.

The venerable Kelley Blue Book has a site, www.kbb.com, which will give you basic vehicle pricing information.

Another site, NADA Appraisal Guides, gives more in-depth pricing on new and used cars. NADA Guides also gives pricing on classic cars; used motorcycles, boats, recreational vehicles, aircraft and mobile homes. You'll find it at www.nadaguides.com.

If you have an idea of what kind of car you want, I highly recommend the eBay Motors Search. It's a search engine just for eBay Motors. Click <u>Search</u> on the top of the eBay Motors page, just below the logo. Then click the tab, Passenger Vehicles, as shown in Figure 18-2.

Using the drop-down menus, click the arrow to select your automobile manufacturer name. This will change the options in the Vehicle Models drop-down menu. Click the arrow to select the model that you are interested in. If you have a preference as to vehicle year, fill in the four-digit year span that you will accept in your search. I suggest that you leave the rest blank so that you get the best idea of what is on the market for your car. Click the Search button, and you'll see all the vehicles up for sale at the time.

Studying the listings

Each listing reflects the personality and the style of the seller. That's one of the fun things about eBay. When you're through reading a listing, you know about the item and about the seller (at least if you're lucky). A brusquely written description may mean you're doing business with someone who won't follow through with the important details.

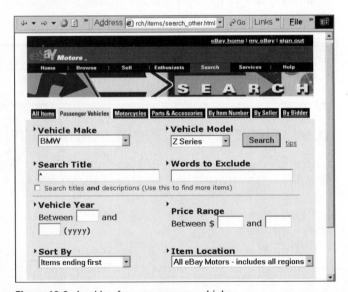

Figure 18-2: Looking for a passenger vehicle.

The listing in Figure 18-3 is from the seller, *e-vehicles*. Note that all eBay Motors listings have an area below the standard feature photo that gives you the *Cliffs Notes* version on facts of the car.

If the car isn't what you're looking for, click the Back button on your browser and look at the next car. eBay has very craftily put the meat of the car details near the top of the listing page, so it won't take forever to work your way through the many car listings.

If the snapshot information passes muster, scroll down to read more. Below the snapshot you'll find the seller's description, and some detailed and clear photographs. Here are the well-written details of *e-vehicles'* description for a Camaro for sale:

> *2000 Chevrolet Camaro Coupe*
>
> *Gold Check Certified one-owner local trade*
>
> *This Gold Check Certified one-owner local trade was purchased and maintained at our area's largest Chevrolet dealership until it was traded in last week. This Medium Red Camaro is equipped with the 200-hp 3.8-liter ohv V6 with automatic overdrive transmission. It also has tilt wheel, AM/FM cassette premium sound, AC, premium wheel covers, ABS, dual airbags, intermittent wipers, rear spoiler, power steering, and dual remote mirrors. There is a full compliment of factory books and a few records in the glove box.*

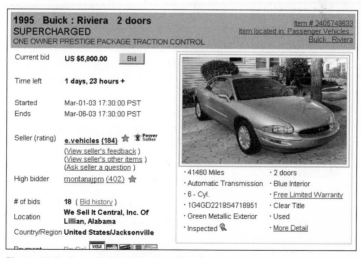

Figure 18-3: A car listing from *e-vehicles*.

Gold Check Certified Pre-Owned Vehicles undergo a 70 item quality-assurance inspection by trained technicians. Gold Check Certified Vehicles are reconditioned in preparation for resale to ensure your satisfaction. It's the next best thing to owning a new vehicle. In addition, I purchased a brand new set of Bridgestone Potenza radials at the time of service. All service is current on this beautiful Camaro.

The car has surprising power and really runs and drives great. The motor, transmission, brakes, and components perform like new. This car has been gently driven and retains that snappy, new-car feel.

The exterior and interior are in fine condition as well. Expect only a few very minor dings and scratches on this awesome Chevy. The interior looks great, but is missing the mat set. The carpets, seats and trim are in excellent condition. This car was previously owned by a non-smoker from McDavid, Florida.

This Chevrolet Camaro has a clean, one-owner background history with no accidents, damage, or discrepancies. The winning bidder will be given a clean title at the time of delivery. The mileage is actual and confirmed.

This seller also runs 12 beautiful photos of the car. He publishes the results of the Carfax title report, reporting a clean title history, and his business philosophy:

My Business Philosophy

My dealership is entirely focused on the sales of vehicles via the eBay format. I make all purchasing and sales decisions and am 100 percent responsible for the content of my auctions. I personally answer every email and conduct all business regarding the sale of this vehicle.

I am a SquareTrade member, which means I have been recognized for my outstanding efforts at attaining customer satisfaction. In addition, eBay recognizes me as a Platinum Level Power Seller.

I buy and list approximately 15-20 units per month.

I look at hundreds of vehicles each week that do not make the cut. . .

This is my living.

I do this full time. I do not have a "car lot." eBay has been my dealership for years, and all operations are focused towards

*bringing you the best vehicle possible at the best price you will
find. I am committed to this format and take your vehicle purchase very seriously. You are dealing with a secure seller.*

The seller then goes on to give the terms of sale, more information
on the transaction and an e-mail address and phone number for
questions. As a buyer, I feel comfortable with this sort of thorough
information.

Seller's terms

Be sure that the seller's terms match your own agenda. If you can't
pick up the car within the next two weeks, and the seller needs it
off his or her property in seven days and won't budge — don't
make the purchase. (Unless you can arrange shipping — or have
someone pick up the car for you — see "Using Motorists Aid for
Purchases," later in this chapter.)

Also, if you want to pay via PayPal, be sure the seller accepts that
form of payment. As always, be sure you read the terms and can
comply.

I know that my constant harangue about feedback ratings can get
mind numbing, but the bigger the purchase the more important
the seller's reputation becomes. How many times can you purchase a car, and get comments from the last 30 or so people
they've done business with? (Be sure, when you're examining the
seller's feedback, to click on the auction number link to be sure the
seller didn't get all the positive feedback for selling *He-Man* VHS
tapes.)

On a purchase as important as this, ask lots of question before you
place your bid. If the seller posts a phone number, be sure to call.
See how you feel about doing business with this person. Once you
place your bid, if you win, it's a binding contract to buy.

Knowing the additional costs

Don't forget that there will be additional costs when you buy your
new car. Your insurance company will be one of the first to jump in
with additional fees, and of course there are license fees.

Need a one-way ticket?

We all know that airlines charge bundles for one-way airfares, and it seems such a waste to buy a round-trip ticket and fly one way. I've got a deal for you! Search eBay for *Southwest Airlines one way*. Frequent flyers who get free flight awards from Southwest don't always use them, and the awards are transferable, but it's not legal to sell them. Crafty eBay sellers sell the drink coupons that come with the free flight coupons and give the air ticket for free! You can get a one-way ticket to anywhere in the country for around $140 — and get a free drink to boot! See Chapter 12 for more on these auctions!

DMV fees

There is a super page online with links to Web sites for the Department of Motor Vehicles for all 50 states (and Washington, D.C.). From your state's home page, you can find out all the required fees, how to get the licenses, and whether personalized plates are available. You'll find the links at http://dmvwebsites.com/.

If you are a member of a local chapter of AAA, check out its Web site before going to the DMV. The Auto Club here in southern California has a direct computer line to the DMV. I went online and got all my information from the DMV and brought it into the auto club; the good people there processed everything I needed, and I never had to stand in the dreaded DMV lines. Check out http://www.aaa.com/scripts/WebObjects.dll/ZipCode.

Finding financing

If you have to get your vehicle financed, eBay has a relationship with eLoan that can approve you if you live in the state of California. Go to http://pages.ebay.com/ebaymotors/services/eLoan-financing.html.

For everyone else in the country, I found PeopleFirst.com online, an online finance company that finances person-to-person transactions for used car loans. I've used PeopleFirst myself and found its service quick and uncomplicated. You can find out more about obtaining a loan from PeopleFirst at www.peoplefirst.com.

Pickup and shipping fees

When you've finally made your deal, it's time to pick up your new baby. Lots of people arrange for auto shipping, and eBay has an alliance with Dependable Auto Shippers. Dependable is, um, *dependable,* and has decades of experience in auto shipping.

Shipping your vehicle can add hundreds of dollars to the cost of your purchase. Isn't it more fun to take a day or two off work and pick up your car? If you must have your car shipped, here's a link to its online quote form `https://www.dasautoshippers.com/ ebay/irate.asp`.

Using your My eBay Watch tab

On a purchase such as this, unless you've found the perfect car right off the bat, you might want to "watch" the bidding on some similar cars. Study when the high bids come in. See what's hot on the eBay market, and what's not. You might just find that your My eBay page can give you the edge, when it comes to buying.

In Chapter 4, I gave you the tour of the My eBay page. On your Bidding/Watching page, you have an area of Items I'm Watching. Figure 18-4 is a section from my Items I'm Watching, featuring some cars that I want to keep an eye on.

Make a note of something very special here. Sellers at eBay Motors have the privilege of lowering their reserves, or Buy It Now prices *during* the auction. This is great for buyers, especially if you're keeping an eye on the bidding. A seller may decide to lower the price, and you can jump right in and catch the deal before anyone else notices!

☐ 2401123761 Chevrolet : Malibu	$4,851.00 42	0d 3h 45m	Bid Now!
☐ 2400856099 Chevrolet : Cavalier	-- --	0d 4h 53m	Bid Now!
☐ 2400856658 Chevrolet : Impala	$6,100.56 16	0d 4h 58m	Bid Now!
☐ 2400865418 Chevrolet : 1939 CHEVY	$23,000.00 19	0d 6h 30m	Bid Now!
☐ 2400890506 Chevrolet : Corvette ⚡Buy It Now	$3,150.00 11	0d 20h 21m	Bid Now!
Good news! Seller has lowered the reserve price. Learn More			
☐ 2400897262 Ford : Thunderbird	$41,600.00 38	0d 22h 15m	Bid Now!
☐ 2400898234 Ford : Thunderbird	$8,600.00 22	0d 22h 23m	Bid Now!

Figure 18-4: Keeping an eye on the bidding without showing your hand.

Picking Up Parts

When I travel around the country teaching at eBay University, I often learn about different ways to make a living by using the eBay venue. The legal chop shop is a recurring theme. Entrepreneurial young (some not so young) men and women around the country attend auto auctions and pick up cars that have been in the worst of car wrecks. These cars are only good for one thing — parts.

So the entrepreneurial shade-tree mechanics bring the cars home, expertly take them apart, screw by screw, and catalog and bag each and every part. Whether you're a collector, home hobbyist, or mechanic, you can take advantage of the low, low prices at eBay, when you're restoring or repairing a car.

When I wanted to bring my 1985 Corvette back to her former glory, I was appalled at the prices I was quoted for parts and labor. I made a list of everything I needed, and approached eBay with caution. Little by little, piece by piece, I purchased almost all the parts I needed from eBay sellers: the interior halo, all the exterior emblems, weather stripping and interior carpeting. I ended up paying about one-third of what it would have cost me locally. I loaded up the car with all the parts (okay, it took several runs) to my trusted mechanic, and he installed all the parts for a low hourly rate. Thanks to the money I saved buying at eBay, I was able to get a beautiful paint job!

When searching for parts at eBay Motors use this search trick, based on the lessons in Chapter 10 to make sure you get the right year for the make and model you're looking for. If you're looking for parts for a 1985 Corvette, for example, type *(85, 1985) Corvette* in the Search box.

Some sellers use the entire year in their title, and others will not.

Using Motorists Aid for Purchases

eBay has gone the distance when it comes to assuring a smooth transaction at eBay Motors. The venue has added features and protection to assure that prudent shoppers have safe transactions. I say prudent because if you are reckless and bid without caution, no one can save you from your own foolishness.

Welcome to the eBay Assurance program

The eBay Assurance program is made up of several parts:

- ✔ **Limited warranty:** A limited warranty is provided to eBay Motors buyers for free on eligible used cars under 10 years old with fewer than 125,000 miles. This limited warranty covers the car for the first month or 1,000 miles (whichever comes first). The warranty covers up to $10,000 in damages, and there is a $500 deductible per visit. For more details and to see which cars are eligible, go to http://pages.ebay. com/ebaymotors/services/warranty.html.

- ✔ **Purchase insurance:** Purchase insurance protects against material fraud or misrepresentation. That's legalese for the big problems, like the odometer being different from the description in the auction, or undisclosed mechanical defects, or perhaps there isn't a clear title to the car; you know — major headaches! The maximum coverage provided is $20,000 with a $500 deductible. The fine print can be found at http:// pages.ebay.com/ebaymotors/services/insurance.html.

- ✔ **Vehicle inspection services:** This would be number one on my list when buying a car from a seller who is miles away from my home. You can schedule a bumper-to-bumper inspection of the car at the seller's location for under $100. Certainly, this could be the best money you'll spend if you can't send your own mechanic to take a look at the car. Pricing and an application are located at http://pages.ebay.com/ebay motors/services/inspection/inspection.html.

- ✔ **Secure Pay by Escrow.com:** A traditional escrow service, where you submit payment to the escrow company, who in turn then tells the seller to ship the vehicle. Once the vehicle arrives at your location and you are satisfied that it is what you purchased, you accept the vehicle, and the escrow company releases the money to the seller. If you want to participate in an escrow, the seller must agree to this type of transaction in advance before you place your bid. The minutiae are at http://pages.ebay.com/ebaymotors/services/ securepay.html.

Protecting yourself

There are a few things you can do to protect yourself before purchasing a vehicle. If the seller hasn't run a Lemon Check on the car, you should. By the way, Lemon Check has become somewhat of a misnomer. The traditional Lemon Check used to merely check to see if the car was identified as a "Lemon" under a stated Lemon Law. Now, a service, CarFax, runs a complete car history check, which has become known as a Lemon Check.

Get the car's VIN number from the top of the eBay auction. Just so you know, the vehicle identification number appears on every car. It's a metal strip, visible on the driver's side through the windshield. Each car has a different number, identifying the characteristics of the vehicle, including manufacturer, year, model, body, engine specifications and serial number. It is assigned at the factory when the car is made.

It is worth the $14.99 to know whether the car has been in any major accidents, or the odometer reading is correct, if it has been salvaged and more. This report will give you the complete car history. If the seller doesn't provide one, go to `http://pages.ebay.com/ebaymotors/services/carfax_lemoncheck.html`.

Chapter 19

Joining the eBay Land Rush

. . . .

In This Chapter

▶ Getting your piece of America

▶ Vacationing in your own resort timeshare

▶ Getting commercial property

▶ Finding bargain foreclosures, homes, and condos

▶ Completing the transaction

. . . .

Since the founding of our country, land has been valued as a great commodity; passed from generation to generation. As Gerald O'Hara so eloquently put it, "it's the only thing that lasts." (Remember that scene from *Gone with the Wind?*) American farmland sprawls across the country, and there's plenty of open space. But because of urbanization and many other factors, large areas of land have had to be subdivided and sold.

People buy land for investment, vacations, or retirement. It's no longer common for a family to spend their entire life in one home. We move and often live in many different places. Real estate, although a major purchase, is becoming more and more an everyday transaction.

The smart people at eBay are sly trend-spotters, so they opened an official category for real estate transactions in fall 2000. You can access eBay's Real Estate category through the category link on the left side of the home page or by going directly to http://www.ebayrealestate.com (see Figure 19-1).

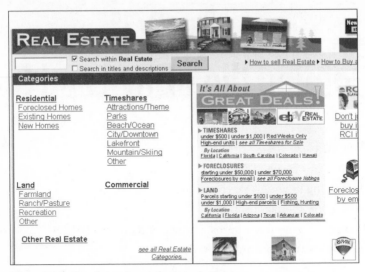

Figure 19-1: Your home for real estate deals.

Because substantial legal restrictions are involved in real estate transactions, sellers can choose to list their properties as an auction or list the property at eBay in the form of an advertisement.

When you participate in a listing that is listed in ad format, you do not place bids. At the bottom of the item's description page, there is a form for you to fill out that sends your information to the seller. Once the seller receives this information, he or she can contact you, and the two of you may negotiate privately. Take a look at Figure 19-2, and you'll see that if we browse the "Residential Homes for sale" category; a small ad icon in the Bids column indicates items that are listed as advertisements.

Most residential home sales are handled in this manner. Land and timeshares are typically sold in the auction format.

Because of a wide variety of laws governing the intricacies and legalities in real estate transactions, the auction may be non-binding. Before getting involved in any real estate transactions at eBay, I suggest you read the official rules; they can be found at `http://pages.ebay.com/help/community/re_agreement.html`.

Residential			Sell in this category

29 items found
Show only: current | new today | **ending today** | going, going, gone

Picture hide	Featured Items - Ending Today	Price	Bids	Time Left
	1996 Ultra Cavalier 3 BR Manufactured Home	$5,100.00	18	1h 28m
	4 Bdrm 2.5 Home Orlando, FL POOL & GOLF	$249,000.00		13h 55m
	LOVELY RANCH STYLE HOME LAKE AREA ON 8 ACRES	$129,000.00		14h 53m

To find out how to be listed in this section and seen by thousands, please visit this link Featured Auctions

Picture	Current Items - Ending Today	Price	Bids	Time Left
	1996 Ultra Cavalier 3 BR Manufactured Home	$5,100.00	18	1h 28m
	Foreclosure: Bethpage TN 37022, 3BD 1BA	$89,900.00		3h 34m
	Mint 4-Bedroom Colonial	$629,900.00		8h 28m

Figure 19-2: Residential homes can be listed in either the Auction or the Ad format.

Getting Your Piece of America

To own a piece of land outright is a great feeling. Whether you plan to live on it or not, just standing on it and knowing that you own it is a great feeling. More and more eBay buyers are getting that feeling. Plenty of virgin land is showing up at eBay in lots and acres on a daily basis.

When shopping for land, as in any real estate transaction, do your research and due diligence. Because most land transactions at eBay are auctions (rather than an ad that is closed by a real estate professional), be sure to read the auction description. Here are some questions you should ask before placing a bid:

> ✔ **Are you bidding on a *down payment* or is it a *straight sale*?** A straight sale is one in which the final bid amount is the total price of the property. If you're bidding a down payment, find out whether the seller will finance the sale, and how much the payments are, what the interest rate will be, and what the other financing terms are.

- ✔ **Is the property buildable?** Is the land level, forested, or rocky? Is there a zoning regulation *requiring* you to build on the property within so many years? Will it allow motor homes (if you're choosing it as a camping location)?

- ✔ **Are there utilities on or nearby the property?** Find out if there's a well. If you need to drill, what is the well depth? Is there a septic tank? Are there paved roads?

- ✔ **How much are the taxes?** Are there any association fees? Are the taxes (and any fees) current?

- ✔ **Is the title guaranteed clear?** What is the legal description (lot number, tract, block)?

- ✔ **How far away is it from civilization?** (Hello? Hello? Hello?)

When you've found a piece of land that you like, do even more research (no matter how nice the seller seems). Say you find some acreage in Billings, Montana. Go to an Internet search engine and type a search for *Billings Montana Assessor.*

When I did this search, the second link that came up in my search gave me the information I was looking for: the Billings, Montana, tax assessor's office. One click and I had the phone number of the assessor's office to check that all property taxes were current. You might also be able to ask the clerk if there is a site that will show you the exact location of the land on a map.

If you want the real lowdown on the area, type the following URL in your browser. Make sure that the last five numbers of this link are the zip code of the area you are interested in, rather than my example of 10022:

```
http://houseandhome.msn.com/pickaplace/nf_details.asp
x?search=1&zip=10022
```

The page that pops up offers demographic information on the area you're interested in. You also see some links on the page to Neighborhood Types, which reveal interesting demographics about the people in the area — even down to the magazines they read!

I confess to having bought land at eBay. Most of it was bought during book research (that's my story, and I'm sticking to it). A look at my diverse real estate holdings gives you a sense of the variety of bargains you can find at eBay:

✔ A postage stamp–size lot in Bakersfield, California (a 26-x-26 foot plot of land, to be exact — but hey, it's mine)

✔ Five acres about 500 feet from the Colorado River in southern Colorado

✔ A 50 foot-x-142 foot lot in Beryl, Utah (because my husband's name is Beryl)

✔ A timeshare in Miami Beach (we already owned another week at the same resort and loved it)

Building a Getaway Home

When you've bought your own little acre, (maybe it's just big enough for a mobile home — but you don't have one of those either) wouldn't you like to be able to visit it — maybe even spend time on it (without having to pitch a tent)?

But you aren't rich enough to be spending money on a second home? Build it yourself! If you're the ambitious type (hey, don't look at me), I've found a very successful seller at eBay who sells some beautiful log cabin homes. No, not like the one ol' Abe Lincoln was born in, but truly beautiful kit homes that are very livable. *Log_Cabin_Home* sells you just about everything you need, and I've seen his prices starting as low as $5,600 (see Figure 19-3).

Figure 19-3: Build your dream home for less money.

You have to install the plumbing, electrical and anything else that is required to abide by your local building codes, but the starter kit is the perfect solution for your getaway home on the piece of land you've just bought at eBay!

Finding Commercial Property

Have you ever thought of just chucking it all, selling everything and starting somewhere else new? If you've never thought of it, just looking over eBay's commercial property (Figure 19-4) might tempt you to do just that.

On the other hand, if you're looking for a great opportunity — a place to start out, this is the place to view your options. Just today, I've found

✔ A coffee shop in Homer, Alaska (the Halibut fishing capital of the world)

✔ An RV park in Colorado

✔ A very lucrative gas station in Kansas (owner has no other choice but to sell)

	NEW FUNERAL HOME	$419,000.00		12d 05h 06m
	BILLBOARD SPACE FOR LEASE INTERSTATE 86 NY	$56.00	18	12d 04h 37m
	Lakefront Resort Plus Acreage/ Avtively Run	$275,000.00	-	12d 04h 25m
	Pharmaceutical Company for Sale	$2,000,000.00		72d 03h 32m
	Montego Bay Jamaica 28 Room Beach Resort	$2,200,000.00		12d 02h 22m
	Remodeled Storefront in Downtown Hillsboro	$150,000.00		12d 00h 14m
	Inn at Magic Mountain, VT Ski Area For Sale	$535,000.00		71d 22h 45m

Figure 19-4: Some of the amazing commercial property for sale at eBay.

> ✔ A boat yard and marina in upstate New York (owner retiring
> after 26 years)
>
> ✔ A profitable turnkey USDA sausage manufacturing plant
> (owner retiring and will train)
>
> ✔ Much, much more

If you have the time, be sure to browse this category; it's a lot of
fun, and you just might find your dream business — and new life.

Of course, there's even more due diligence involved when you're
buying a business than when you're bidding on a plot of land. An
accountant and a lawyer should be involved in transactions such
as these. Most of the transactions in this category are listed in the
ad format; you send your information to the seller and negotiate
offline. If the business is an auction, be sure to contact the seller to
get all questions asked before bidding.

Buying Residential Property

Residential real estate is divided into several categories. You can
buy homes and condos for sale by private parties, and get a bargain in the process by saving the large percentage that is tradition-
ally charged by full-service brokers.

I spoke to my local broker, and he unquestionably agreed about
the savings. Real estate brokers spend lots of time marketing properties that may never sell because sellers may have unrealistic
expectations of how much they can get for their properties.
Putting a property up for sale at eBay gives sellers a good idea of
how much work is involved in selling their property. eBay's a win-
win venue for both the buyer and the seller. A professional broker
does need to step in, of course, when it comes to closing the deal.
Disclosure statements, title searches and those sticky legalities are
best left to professionals, but these services will come at a much
lower price — once the deal has been struck at eBay.

Finding new and custom homes

Who'd have thought that new home developers would have turned
to eBay to sell their homes? They always have those fancy furnished

models, well-dressed sales people and fine brochures. Who would even believe they'd think that little old eBay could help them sell their homes. Ha! Those guys and gals at eBay have always been smart like foxes, and they also know a good thing when they see it. How else can they expose their homes to 49 million people for a few hundred dollars in listing fees?

In this subcategory of real estate, you'll find listings by developers whose homes are in the planning, building and selling stages. You'll be able to look at the plans and contact the builders. Browsing this category is just like viewing model homes.

Finding Foreclosures

Finding foreclosures at eBay isn't difficult, but it is certainly not a mission for the amateur. You will find several types of foreclosures. Some are sold by the lender (an individual or a bank) and some are being sold by HUD (no, not Paul Newman), the U.S. Department of Housing and Urban Development; or the VA (Veterans Administration). To make an offer on a foreclosed property, you must have a licensed real estate agent make the offer for you. If you currently don't work with a broker, eBay has a page that will help you find a broker experienced in these types of transactions. You will find it at `www.ebayrealestate.net/find_agent_f.htm`.

HUD and VA homes, contrary to urban legend, cannot be purchased for a dollar. They can be quite a bargain, and generally are sold at market value, but in an "as-is" state, without warranty. The agencies realize that repairs may have to be made to these properties, and the asking price reflects this fact.

In many states, HUD or the VA may pay all, or a portion of, closing or financing costs as well as sales commission. It is up to the agent to negotiate this for the buyer.

These homes should be professionally inspected so that all needed repairs will be known *prior* to making an offer on the property.

Foreclosed homes are sold in an *offer period*. At the end of the period, all bids are opened, and the property is sold to the highest reasonable bid. If the home isn't sold within the initial period, bids may be submitted 24 hours a day, 7 days a week, and will be opened the next business day. When HUD or the VA finally accepts a bid, the submitting broker is notified within approximately 48 hours.

If you're hooked on the idea of foreclosures and you'd like to get the listings the minute eBay receives them, you can sign up for e-mail notification by going to www.ebayrealestate.net/ prop_email_f.htm.

Bidding on Vacation Timeshares

Ok, here's where you can sign me up. I like the idea of knowing that I'm forced to go to a beautiful condo on the beach for the same week every year. No matter what. It's my week, my week in the sun. Owning my timeshare guarantees that I get at least one weekend away each year. True, I often have to take my laptop and complete a few chapters, but heck, I do them from a lounge chair (with piña colada in hand) on the beach in Miami! I know, I know. It's no fun living the life of a starving writer (see Figure 19-5).

Some people like to buy timeshares for their *trading power*. There are organizations like RCI (Resort Condominiums International) that will take *your* week at *your* timeshare in trade for a different week at another timeshare at any of its inventory of close to 4,000 resorts worldwide! Some of my friends have never even visited their home timeshare; they just keep trading!

Your Own Beachfront Getaway!

Invest in the most beautiful vacation spot in the country, Miami Beach - right on the ocean. Buy at today's prices and you can come back to this
luxurious resort the same week every year. All fees are current with mortgage paid in full. Your vacation begins this year, 2003. This prime, RCI Red resort has maximum trading power giving you the ability to choose from over 3,700 resorts worldwide, should you ever decide to bank or exchange your week.
This is a beautifully decorated, 2 and 1/2 bath lock-off unit that has a lovely living room (with sofa bed), dining area, master and guest bedrooms, (Master bathroom features a jacuzzi tub), full kitchen & two terraces with ocean view. Occupancy and privacy for 6 persons. We currently own two weeks at this resort and we love going - so will you!

Figure 19-5: This piece of the tropics sold for around $2,800 at eBay.

I think we've all heard of someone who has attended a high-pressure timeshare presentation for a new timeshare. They not only had high pressure but high prices. Sadly, the person who first buys a new timeshare pays the highest price — he or she is covering the resort developer's marketing and advertising costs. Once the unit goes up for resale at eBay, the bargain is yours. Here are a few things to check on when you consider buying a timeshare at eBay:

- ✔ **Find out if the timeshare is fixed week or floating:** The year is broken up into 52 numbered weeks, and the weeks usually start on a Saturday. In a *fixed-week* arrangement, you purchase a particular week, and that week's reserved for you each year. To find out when, say, week 22 lands in the more-typical monthly calendar, go to a search engine such as Yahoo! or Google and search for *timeshare calendar.*

  A *floating week* usually starts on a Friday, Saturday, or Sunday and goes on a first come, first served basis. The week you spend in the timeshare may vary from year to year; what your purchase price is based on is size and quality of the unit rather than time of year. If you want a specific week during high season, you'd best book it with the resort far in advance.

- ✔ **Find out if the timeshare is certificate or deeded:** Ownership within the United States is typically *deeded* or *fee simple.* This means that you own your interest in the resort. You get a deed and you can pass it on to your heirs. A *certificate* or *leased* timeshare gives you the right to use the timeshare for a pre-scribed amount of years, usually 25 to 30. These are common outside the United States.

- ✔ **Find out the occupancy and how private the timeshare is:** Maximum is the number of guests the resort will accommodate, private occupancy is the number of guests that can be accom-modated (based on two adults) with a private bathroom.

- ✔ **Find out what the maintenance fees are like:** There are annual maintenance fees paid to the resort. Somebody has to pay for the upkeep, the utility bills, the taxes, insurance, cable TV, and so on. Just like home.

To learn more about timeshares, visit one of the Internet's oldest and largest membership sites, Timeshare Users Group. I visit it often and I highly recommend the site; it's loaded with reviews on resorts and recommendations. Visit `http://www.tug2.net/`.

Chapter 20

Getting Glitzy

In This Chapter

▶ Finding great savings on jewelry

▶ Shopping that's more convenient than a mall

▶ Finding men's basics without the hassle

You wouldn't know it by what I'm wearing now — but I adore fashion. I love wearing new clothes and accessories — there's very little that feels better than going somewhere in a brand new outfit. Wait a minute, yes there is, it's when you pay less than half of retail for your clothes and accessories.

I don't earn enough money to support my fashion habit in the way I'd truly like, but once more, eBay gives us the opportunity to get on the glitz — without breaking the bank. In Chapter 13, I show you how eBay helps you purchase wedding gowns at a sixth of the retail price — and yes, this same kind of savings extends into all areas of fashion — for both men and women.

Finding Sparkling Savings on Jewelry

When I talk about shopping (or even selling) at eBay, I always tell people to buy (or sell) what they know. If you know nothing about what you're looking for, there's a far better chance of you spending way too much for an item.

Finding fine jewelry

If you're looking for a specific type of piece, like an engagement ring, I suggest you go to some retail stores before you browse eBay. Get an idea of what you like. What catch phrases does the jeweler use to describe your ring? Understand cut and clarity before you go bidding up a ring at eBay.

Once you know what you're looking for, spend time going through the eBay listings. Odds are you will find exactly what you want — for considerably less than Ms. Jeweler wanted to sell it to you for.

When you plan to buy a special piece of jewelry at eBay, there are a few things to keep in mind:

- ✔ **E-mail the seller:** More likely than not, some of your questions won't be answered in the item description. Ask the seller. You have the right to expect a quick and respectful reply. A good seller will treat you as a good customer, and will respond to your e-mail quickly.

- ✔ **Check the seller's feedback:** Is the seller an established jewelry seller? Or does his or her background refer to selling hundreds of low-cost items? If you're dealing with an established seller who sells an occasional piece of jewelry, or an established jewelry seller, you can probably trust the feedback rating. If not, try another auction. (Check on the auction links to see what the sellers have been selling.)

- ✔ **Look for a warranty or a legitimate appraisal:** Once the seller has passed your feedback inspection, see if he or she offers a guarantee that the description is correct. Also determine whether the seller will refund your money upon return of the product if you discover a problem with the item.

- ✔ **Ask for additional pictures:** If you're spending hundreds (or even thousands) of dollars, you have the right to have clear pictures of the item. If the auction does not have enough pictures, ask the seller to e-mail you some more.

Figure 20-1 shows an auction from the eBay store *One Source Gems* for some stunning diamond and platinum stud earrings at eBay.

Note the way the seller gave a complete and thorough description of the item for sale, and guaranteed the purchase.

Jewelry Information	
Inv. ID: SP-PRSE050-P	
Metal Type : Platinum	
Carats: 1/2ctw	
Color: F	
Clarity: VVS2	
Stones: 2 Matching Princess Diamonds	
Set Type : Prong	
Mounting: Basket setting with screw-on backs.	
Retail Value: $1,999.00	
OSG Price : No Reserve!	

These diamond stud earrings are guaranteed to be beautiful! The diamonds are handselected for beauty, matched and then set in a beautiful Platinum basket mounting with screw-on backs. The diamond have a VERY WHITE F color and a VVS2 clarity! These diamonds are VERY WHITE & VERY BRIGHT! The diamonds also have a beautiful cut! They have lots of fire & are very sparkly! We guarantee these Diamond Stud Earrings to be what we say AND to be beautiful! These will

These earrings come accompanied by the following complimentary items:

- Beautiful Cherry Wood Gift Box
- Detailed Appraisal.
- Fully Insured FedEx 2-Day Shipping (2-Day in 48 states) .
- Shipped and delivered within 5 business day of receipt of payment.

Figure 20-1: These earrings from seller *quality@onesourcegems. com* were appraised for $1,999 and sold for $600.

If you're looking for lower-price "fun" (but real) jewelry, know how much you'd spend for that item in a retail store. Then go online and have fun. Just know your budget *before* you bid.

eBay has a very active Discussion Board about jewelry. You can ask questions there and you may get an expert answer — or not. Realize that just because people sell a type of item, it doesn't make them true experts. I have sold jewelry in the past (and know quite a deal about it), but am certainly not an expert! Visit the Jewelry discussion board for ideas at: http://forums.ebay.com/db0/ forum.jsp?forum=32.

Finding classic and new watches

There is virtually no better place on earth to buy watches than eBay! The prices are really discounted, and you can compare brand and model to original retail. When you research your buying in this manner, you know exactly what you're getting.

Watches are also something that you should be careful about when you buy. Check the seller's feedback and follow all the caveats listed above for fine jewelry.

There is also a fantastic market for classic fine watches at eBay. But then again, if you don't know anything about classic watches, there is a chance you can pay more than you need to. If you're looking for a classic watch, there are several very thorough reference books (that are sold at eBay) that will teach you the background and history of the watch you've got your eye on. These books also give you the key to the serial numbers and models, so that when you see an auction you'll have a better idea of what you're looking at, and know what questions to ask the seller. Check out Figure 20-2 to see what kinds of steals you can find.

Bidding on vintage and new costume jewelry

These days, costume jewelry is as collectible (if not more) as fine jewelry. A few years ago, the famous designer (and very rich lady) Gloria Vanderbilt had her "garage sale" of her extra costume jewelry at eBay. She'd collected many famous items throughout the years and sold them to regular folks like you and me. It was from her auctions that I learned about the classic jewelry designers. Check out Figure 20-3 for a beautiful costume jewelry find.

Picture	Item Title	Price	Bids	Time Left
	LIKE NOS ROLEX SS DATE OYSTER ROMAN WATCH NR!	$1,175.00	35	1m
	NEW!! ROLEX DATEJUST QUARTZ WATCH w/BOX&PAPER	$2,400.00 $2,800.00 =Buy It Now	-	1m
	ROLEX OYSTER PERPETUAL DATEJUST	$1,425.00 $3,995.00 =Buy It Now	23	1m
	18K ROLEX DATEJUST LADIES WATCH NO RESERVE!	$1,005.00	25	1m
	ROLEX MEN SS OYSTER PERP DATEJUST WATCH SLVR	$1,495.00	-	2m
	ROLEX LADIES 18K PRESIDENT WATCH DIAMONDS	$6,995.00	-	3m
	MENS ROLEX 18k/SS OYSTER PERP DATE WATCH GOLD	$2,095.00	-	3m
	Rolex, Ladies 14K , Elegantly	$1,200.00	-	7m

Figure 20-2: I searched for *Rolex* and netted close to 2,000 watches.

Finest Costume
Designed Jewelry

You are looking at a brand new Victorian styled Flower Necklace set. This beautiful necklace set is made of Siam, Siam AB and Garnet colored Genuine Austrian Crystals and Acrylic Beads set in an Antique Rhodium tone. The necklace measures 15" long to an adjustable 18". The earrings are for pierced ears and measure 1/3"W x 7/8"L aprox. All our items are gift boxed. Good luck~~~!

Figure 20-3: Stunning new necklace from seller *superpriceonline.*

Famous brands, jewelry designed by Miriam Haskell, Kenneth J. Lane, Dior, Weiss, and Lisner all command high prices at eBay. Today's designers of elegant costume jewelry, like Joan Rivers, Judith Mack, and Nolan Miller are appearing on the site and are quickly growing in value.

The watch that didn't come in

My husband visited our "family" jeweler. You know, the guy who you trust and go over to when you want something special and you don't want to get ripped off; the jeweler you trust. Interestingly, both my husband and I treated this same jeweler as our "family" jeweler before we even met each other — so we both really trust him.

Anyway, my husband went into the store and found a super-looking watch — and bought it. It was one of those new Citizen Eco-Drive watches (the kind where the crystal is a solar cell, and you don't have to replace batteries). The jeweler showed my husband a picture of a stunning ladies watch of the same type, in gold with diamond accents.

My husband didn't order it (luckily) and came home to tell me about it. I searched eBay and found the exact watch — brand new, still in the box — for *half* the *discounted off-retail* price our jeweler would have sold it to my husband for when it came in. I don't dare wear the watch when I visit our "family" jeweler, but I'm darn proud that I got such a deal!

Finding Mall Fashion from Your Home

If there is one category that I visit more than any other at eBay, it's fashion. Everything you wear, from elegant men's suits to mink coats, can be found here at incredible discounts. Not everything you find online is used stuff either — over 52 percent of items listed in this category at eBay are brand new.

All you have to know is that an item exists, and you can find it here. In 2002, there were $420 million dollars in sales in the eBay apparel category alone. The people who run the eBay apparel category tell me that:

✔ A pair of Nike shoes sells every 2 minutes.

✔ A Coach handbag sells every 4 minutes.

✔ A pair of Levi's jeans sells every 1.5 minutes.

Those are some pretty amazing figures. Seems that the fashion *cognoscenti* are seriously shopping for their fashion at eBay.

Be sure you know your size in a particular brand when you buy it at eBay. When I search eBay for certain brands, I know what size I wear, so there's no mystery when the item arrives as to whether it will fit.

Women's apparel

From top to bottom it's here at eBay. Here you can find lots (as in a *lot* — a single item for several of the same thing) of brand new lingerie. All things we like to buy in multiples!

Not only that, but clothing and shoes of every make and designer are here. As a matter of fact, the second most searched search term at eBay is *Gucci!*

When you go to the <u>Clothing and Apparel</u> link from the eBay home page, you'll end up on the hub page shown in Figure 20-4.

Figure 20-4: The eBay Clothing, Shoes, and Accessories hub page.

Ladies, there's lots of stuff you can be buying here:

✔ **Lingerie:** Did you know that the waitresses at Hooters wear special pantyhose that help their gorgeous legs look even better? Well, they do, and guess what — we can buy them at eBay! (Without ever having to go into Hooters — *shudder*). Speaking of pantyhose, did you know they make pantyhose without feet (so that you can stay smooth but still wear sandals?). Yep, they're called Spanx, and they cost around $20 in stores, but you can buy them brand new at eBay for close to half price.

There are also lots and lots of Victoria's Secret closeout, new merchandise on the site. And don't forget misspellings! I just ran the search *victories secret* and got 1,832 items!

✔ **Nightwear:** Name brand pajamas like Karen Neuberger, and Nick and Nora are awfully pricey and hard to find in stores — at eBay they are plentiful and go at big discounts!

✔ **Casual wear:** If Levi's sell so quickly — you can imagine how fast the Tommy Bahama or Jam's World items sell. That is when you can find just the one you want!

✔ **Designer dresses:** If you know the brand, you can find the designer at eBay. No matter where they are from or what they sell! Search by manufacturer's name, as I sit here I've searched a bunch of popular brands; ABS, Due per Due, Moschino, Banana Republic — you name it. I found items from each one at eBay!

✔ **Shoes and purses:** You can find every major designer's merchandise at eBay at prices most of us can afford. When it comes to shoes, be sure you know your size before you buy! Many shoe auctions are final. Where else can you get a *new* pair of Jimmy Choo or Manolo Blahnik shoes for under $100?

I could keep on listing items, but I think you've gotten the idea. You can find whatever you want from Target's Mossimo to Neiman's Lulu Guinness!

Lots of very popular manufacturers are opening stores at eBay for overruns and surplus inventory. Lately I've seen stores by Clio (store name: *1010 Direct*) and Chadwick's Outlet, but there are many more. Be sure to run your favorite designer's name through the store search as well as the eBay search so you'll get all the bargains. See more on stores in Chapter 15.

Once you get your favorite sellers and stores, you can store their names on your favorites list in your My eBay page. Then, with a click of the mouse, you can see what's for sale. Figure 20-5 shows a tiny section of what I found from one of my favorite stores.

[$ 88 Now sz small Shirt](#)	$4.99	-	3 hours, 53 mins +
[$ 88 Now sz small Shirt](#)	$4.99	1	3 hours, 53 mins +
[$ 40 Style and company sz xx-large Shirt](#)	$4.99	-	3 hours, 54 mins +
[$ 88 Escapades sz 14 Shirt](#)	$4.99	1	3 hours, 54 mins +
[$ 46 Style and company sz xx-large Shirt](#)	$4.99	1	3 hours, 54 mins +
[$ 40 Charter Club sz medium Sweater](#)	$4.99	-	3 hours, 54 mins +
[$ 9 Alfani sz x-small Shirt](#)	$4.99	1	3 hours, 54 mins +

Figure 20-5: Items closing today in the *evalueville* store.

Getting men's basics without the hassle

If most men are like my husband, they really don't like to go shopping. If my husband needs shirts, he'll go to the store and find a shirt he likes and then buy it in every color. Same thing with shoes. It doesn't really make for a fashion-forward look. I've found that I can go onto eBay and select some really great looks for him. I usually just slip the new stuff — as it arrives from the seller — directly into his closet!

On the other hand, some men just love to shop — and you guys will really like eBay. Just plug in your favorite designers or manufacturer, and just like the women's clothes, you'll find way more than you need or want! Take a look at Figure 20-6. This item is from the seller *gothamcityonline,* who lists hundreds (maybe thousands) of items for men and women daily. I often shop its stuff for myself, but it has an awesome selection for men!

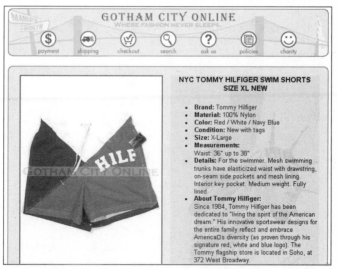

Figure 20-6: *Gothamcityonline's* great deal on Tommy Hilfiger swim shorts.

Part VII
The Part of Tens

The 5th Wave   By Rich Tennant

"Guess who found a KISS merchandise blowout at eBay while you were gone?"

In this part...

What *For Dummies* book would be complete without The Part of Tens? I won't buck tradition. Visit this part for fun buying tips from people who know (sellers)! I also give you a taste of the variety, humor, diversity, and fun that make so many people so loyal to the eBay community. Welcome to our club. Happy bargain hunting!

Chapter 21

Ten Things eBay Sellers Want You to Know

. . . .

*H*ave you ever had something that you wanted to tell someone that was so very important that you couldn't stress it enough? Something really earthshaking? (Like telling your kids that the sick they feel after they get drunk is *really* not worth it.) I wanted to name this chapter; "Ten Things Sellers Would Like to Tell Buyers While Grabbing You by the Shoulders and Shaking You Violently." So now you know, these are very important tips to being a successful shopper at eBay.

I e-mailed quite a few truly reliable sellers for suggestions for this chapter. Not necessarily the big sellers, but the sellers who know what they are doing. The ones with excellent feedback and quality customer service.

All these sellers want to deal with savvy, smart, and informed shoppers, and they want you to trust all sellers, which means that they want you to ask questions, be suspicious, and above all, remember: If something sounds like it's too good to be true, it probably is.

Identify Your Payment

Every eBay seller who has been selling on the site for any length of time has received payments that they couldn't possibly identify. One of the sellers I spoke to about this chapter just received a money order with no identification information. It was bought for $16.94 and never signed or filled out, no eBay item number. Nothing.

That's why sellers suggest that you print your e-mail exchange or a copy of the auction and send it with your payment. Be sure that every payment you send has the following information:

- ✔ The item name and number
- ✔ Your eBay User ID
- ✔ The address the item is to be shipped to
- ✔ Remind the seller if you want the item to be sent insured

Without this information, a seller can't be expected to send your item to you in a prompt manner.

Also, *print* your information, deciphering someone's handwriting is a very specialized talent.

Check Feedback Before You Bid

eBay has a great tool, the seller's box on the item page, which tells you the percentage of positive feedback a seller has received. But that box just gives you a summary. To get the complete picture, you must click the number after the seller's name or the Read All Reviews in the line below the seller's ID.

Check to be sure that the leopard didn't change his stripes (or was that the zebra?). Be sure that the last few feedbacks are not negative, and that the negatives are for dangerous situations. Look for red flags, such as references to non-shipment of items and non-response to e-mail after a payment. *Read* the negatives.

If a seller has some negative feedback, be sure to go through it. See if the seller isn't in the clear because the feedback is followed up with an update that says `Oops. Sorry for leaving negative feedback. The item arrived safely. Thank you.` (For more information on feedback, see Chapter 5.)

Take a Time-Out Before Leaving Negative Feedback

Has your package not arrived as yet? Did the item arrive and it wasn't exactly as you expected it? Was the item damaged in transit, and is there no clue on the package that the seller purchased insurance for the shipment (as you requested?). Take a deep breath and count to ten.

Before you start drafting a short, stinging feedback message, communicate with the seller. E-mail the seller immediately. Politely, please.

Don't get emotional; just state your case and give the seller the opportunity to make things right for you.

If e-mail is too slow (even though it's best *not* to communicate while you're seething), go to eBay's search page and click the Find Members link to (from the Navigation Bar at the top of the page). Scroll down to the contact info area. Input the item number for the transaction, as well as the seller's User ID — and click Submit.

eBay e-mails you the seller's telephone number, and your number will go to the seller.

Just like for our government, diplomacy will work for you. Most sellers (you *did* check their feedback *before* you bid, right?) will bend over backwards for their customers so as to protect their reputation at eBay.

Give the seller the chance to make your transaction a pleasant one. Don't permanently ruin his or her online reputation because you got caught up in the moment. For the first 24 hours after you get an item, practice your deep breathing techniques and believe only the best about the seller you're working with. Give him or her a chance to respond positively.

About 90 percent of negative feedback is given by newbies. Be in the top 10 percent of your class!

Check for an eBay Store

When you've decided to buy a Buy It Now item, or bid on a seller's auction, double-check to see if the seller has an eBay store. Look for the small red store tag after the seller's name. If he or she has an eBay store, click on the red tag, and you'll be taken to the seller's store. Sellers often list the very same items in their eBay store for a lower Buy It Now price. Why? It costs them considerably less to list items in their store, and they list more items.

Once you're in the store see if the seller has the items you want listed in their store as Buy It Now items. (You wouldn't see these items listed on an eBay search.) Just type a keyword from the item title in the search box in the store. You can save money by clicking your mouse, and taking an extra minute. It's definitely worth it.

Purchase Multiple Items from a Seller

If you've found an item you want to buy, or if you've just won an auction, be sure to click on the link in the seller's box that says View Seller's Other Items. Often, sellers sell other items related to the one you've just won, and you may just find something else that appeals to you. If the seller had the good taste to sell a certain type of item, perhaps he or she has other like interests as you do.

If you see another item you want, be sure to e-mail the seller saying that you would like the items shipped together, and ask the seller to give you the amount due for combined shipping.

Also, if you intend to pay via PayPal, ask the seller to send you a combined PayPal invoice. If you pay for each item individually, the seller will incur extra, unnecessary charges from PayPal for multiple transactions — rather than for one combined sale.

Be Vigilant When Using Escrow

Most eBay transactions go through without a problem. But sadly, one of the easiest places for fraud to occur when you're buying online is when you are purchasing the most expensive of items. Buyers and sellers can often save themselves a bunch of grief if they run their high-dollar transaction through an escrow company.

Here's the rub. The Internet has been inundated with make-believe escrow companies. Unscrupulous sellers will set up a Web site with information copied from a real escrow site, and act as an escrow company. They take your money *and* keep the merchandise (if it ever even belonged to them).

Smart, honest sellers want you to know about the scammers — better-educated bidders will seek out only the finest sellers, thus drumming up more business for the good guys.

Because you're doing business at eBay, double-check on the eBay site which escrow service they are recommending at the time. Go to the eBay site `http://pages.ebay.com/help/community/escrow.html`. Escrow.com is currently the escrow site of choice for eBay transactions.

Be especially wary if a seller *insists* on using an escrow service because it's usually the buyer that insists on escrow — *not* the seller.

If You Worry About Receiving Packages

A sad result of the problems in this day and age is that we are often uncomfortable receiving unmarked packages. Even though you may be expecting an eBay purchase in the mail, you may look with worry at a particular package.

Ask the seller to e-mail you when he or she ships the package with information as to how the package is being shipped. If he or she is using delivery confirmation, ask for that number to be sent to you in the shipping confirmation e-mail.

The good ones will not blink. They'll just do their best to accommodate you.

Please, Read the Description

When you are interested in an item, be sure to read the description. Some sellers do have overly long descriptions, and it's a pain to read the entire thing. But if you are interested in buying an item, you must slog through the entire thing to be sure you know about the item and are comfortable with the shipping and terms of sale.

Many times sellers get e-mails (I am guilty of sending these e-mails, too!) asking questions that are answered in the item description. Buyers often miss out on great deals because they were waiting for an answer that was given in the description.

 Also be sure you are comfortable with the shipping amount. If the shipping amount is not listed, e-mail the seller by clicking the Ask Seller a Question link. Ask the seller how much shipping would be to your zip code. Shipping cost is part of the cost of your item and you have a right to decide whether you feel it is reasonable, before you place a bid.

If you have more questions about an item's condition or value (or that photographs are accurate) be sure to get confirmation from the seller via the e-mail link *before* placing your bid.

Know What You're Bidding On

Educated bidders are more fun (and less time-consuming) for sellers to deal with. And unless you don't worry about wasting money, it's smart for you to know about the item you want to buy. Here's what you should know:

- ✔ **If it is an item you can currently buy at a local store, but buying at eBay is more convenient, be sure you're not paying too much of a premium for having it delivered to your door.** Call your local store and see if it has it and how much it is.

- ✔ **If the item is an article of clothing, be sure it is the size you require.** You can ask the seller if that brand runs large or small, but it's best to buy brands with whose sizes you are familiar. Also, if you don't like going to the dry cleaner, e-mail the seller to see if the item is washable.

- ✔ **Don't assume the item is new unless the seller says so.**

- ✔ **If the item is a collectible, be sure that it is as rare as you think it is.** Run an eBay search on completed items to see how many sold within the last two weeks at eBay, and see how much other buyers paid.

Beware of Unsolicited Offers

Your bids at eBay are public record, and anyone can tell what you are bidding on (unless it is a private auction). Sometimes sellers scour the auctions and contact bidders to sell them a similar — or exactly the same — item for a lower price. Rather than putting their items up for sale, and paying eBay fees, these unscrupulous sellers choose to undercut other reputable seller's sales.

By participating in this bidder-stealing practice, sellers can avoid paying fees to eBay. Sadly, if you choose to accept one of these off-eBay transactions, you are not protected under the eBay Fraud Protection Program and cannot use the eBay feedback system. You are completely on your own.

If you find this form of solicitation annoying, you can report the user to eBay through the Customer service e-mail reporting link (http://pages.ebay.com/help/basics/select-RS.html).

The quickest way to contact eBay Customer Support is to click a feedback star anywhere on the eBay site and scroll to the bottom of the page that appears. Then click the link.

It is a violation of eBay policy for a seller to solicit sales, and sellers may be suspended for using this tactic.

Chapter 22

Ten Really Great Things About Shopping at eBay

1 could come up with a bunch of reasons that shopping at eBay is fun, or special or even sensible. I'm not the average eBay shopper. Since I've begun writing books about eBay in 1999, eBay has become a big part of my life.

Writing, teaching at eBay University, consulting — yes, eBay definitely takes up time. I finally gave up a very successful marketing and advertising business so that I could devote the appropriate amount of time to eBay — and my readers.

But I really enjoy it. I love the buyers and sellers; I love testing new marketing ideas on the site; seeing people's businesses grow. I hear from people when they are about to start an eBay business — and I love to hear from them again when they're successful. That's happened more times than I can count.

So I'd like to start off this chapter by saying that the first great thing (for me) about shopping at eBay is that it changed my life. It's done that for many people who have changed careers and are selling at eBay. Part-time businesses became good sized — even large. So thank you, eBay.

I contacted some more of my fellow eBay shoppers to find out what they find is special about shopping on the site. So here are ten (or so) reasons to shop at eBay.

You Can Find More Choices Than at the Mall

When you log on to eBay to find something, odds are you'll think of something else you want. There are close to 10,000,000 items up for sale each and every day on the site. New things, old things, used things and rare things. There are items to drive, vacations to go to and items to wear.

You can find something to make anyone happy at eBay — because it is all there. From welding kits to wedding gowns, signed first editions to new books hot off the press. You can buy the toy you always wanted as a kid, that your parents wouldn't (or couldn't afford to) buy. You can buy your child the book you treasured in school that you could never find again.

If you stretch your imagination, you can come up with (and find) the most outrageous of items that you never even thought existed. It's all for sale; from birth to death; at eBay.

This Mall Never Closes

You can shop at eBay at any hour of any day. If you can't sleep at night, you can look for the replacement filter for your air conditioner at 2:30 in the morning.

You Don't Need to Dress Up

No one cares if you're in your pajamas or in a tuxedo — although I know of no eBay shoppers that shop in their tuxedos. (If you do, please drop me a line.) Most of the buyers and sellers prefer a more casual look. But then it makes no difference — it's just you and the Internet.

You Don't Have to Deal with Pushy Sales People

Okay, I guess if you've read enough descriptions at eBay auctions you do notice that *some* sellers can be a bit pushy. Maybe not just some and maybe not just a bit.

But the best part of eBay is that if you don't like the attitude the seller projects in his or her text, you can click your mouse and find a nicer, friendlier seller selling your item.

You Can Shop the World Over

If you're looking for an item from another country, you *might* find it at eBay. But if you go to one of the international sites:

Argentina, Australia, Austria, Belgium, Brazil, Canada, France, Germany, Ireland, Italy, Korea, Mexico, the Netherlands, New Zealand, Singapore, Spain, Sweden, Switzerland, Taiwan, and the United Kingdom

You might get closer to finding just what you're looking for. (I find my favorite ketchup potato chips at eBay Canada.) You might even try searching the foreign sites for old recipes and more.

To get to the international sites on the eBay home page, scroll down the page. The links to the sites are in the lower left-hand corner of links, just below the categories.

You're Joining a Community

The eBay community, via the chat rooms and discussion boards, can become a whole second social life for members who spend time there. People meet at pre-assigned hours, and discuss eBay and world events. It's like a town square — just find one you like and join in.

You can visit international boards as well. I enjoy visiting the United Kingdom boards. I have family over there, and it's nice to meet people from other countries. If you speak foreign languages, you can join the fun at the international eBay site's chat rooms. You won't find them in every country — but give it a try. eBay is always adding new features.

You Can Give Back to Non-Profit Organizations

You can have more fun buying very unique things, and the money goes to charity. There are many charitable organizations that are selling their wares at eBay to raise money for their fine work. You can get some very rare and unusual items here, like the annual NBC *Today Show* Green Room autograph book. This one-of-a-kind book has signatures and notes from the famous guests of the *Today Show*. The 2002 edition was sold in January 2003 and had over 500 autographs. It sold for $27,100 and benefited the Boys and Girls Clubs of America.

eBay recently partnered with the leader in online charitable auctions, MissionFish. Since 2000, MissionFish has helped organizations turn donations into cash through online auctions. MissionFish will be working with regular eBay sellers to raise money for non-profit organizations.

Late in 2003, sellers will begin to be able to pick a benefiting non-profit from a certified list, and designate a percentage of the proceeds (from 20 to 100 percent) to donate, when they list an item at eBay. These items will appear in the search results with a Charity Auction icon. When you go to the item page, you'll see the name of the non-profit and some information about it, and the percentage of the final bid that the seller is donating. You can search eBay for your favorite non-profits by name.

You Can Use the eBay Toolbar

If you really get into eBay and want to keep track of items, and have an instant link to eBay — at any time — you might want to download the eBay Toolbar. The eBay Toolbar becomes part of your Internet browser and allows you to connect to eBay at the click of your mouse. See Figure 22-1 to see it in action.

Figure 22-1: My eBay Toolbar, revealing my drop-down Watch list.

You search eBay for anything that pops into your mind by typing it into the small search box and clicking Search eBay. You can click on any of the blocks to get to your bidding and Watch list.

Figure 22-2 shows the small box that pops up in the corner of your screen 10 minutes before your watched auction closes to give you a chance to snipe!

You can download the toolbar for your computer at http://pages. ebay.com/ebay_toolbar/.

Figure 22-2: Excuse me —
time to click here to snipe.

You Can Express Yourself

A new hobby has hit the Internet. Not just the one about passing on wacky, joke e-mails, it's passing on links to wacky auctions. Has anyone sent you an e-mail showing you something strange up for sale at eBay? Well, once you get onboard, and have friends who also use eBay, you'll be treated to some gems of madcap auctions.

Most of those auctions that you read about in the newspaper or hear about on TV are real. Here are a few of the recent auction titles:

Invisible Gold Fish — Matched Pair

PANCREAS COFFEE MUG . . . IT'S WEIRD & WONDERFUL!

Paper Origami Boulder

Nudist family activities needlepoint. Framed

FOR SALE: 24 SMALL CHILDREN

Fully functional kidney for donation

Young Man's Virginity. Please look

Of course, some were in violation of eBay policy and ended by the site; others were just plain funny!

Index

• **F** •

FOR DUMMIES®

The easy way to get more done and have more fun

PERSONAL FINANCE

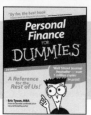

0-7645-5231-7   0-7645-2431-3   0-7645-5331-3

Also available:

Estate Planning For Dummies (0-7645-5501-4)

401(k)s For Dummies (0-7645-5468-9)

Frugal Living For Dummies (0-7645-5403-4)

Microsoft Money "X" For Dummies (0-7645-1689-2)

Mutual Funds For Dummies (0-7645-5329-1)

Personal Bankruptcy For Dummies (0-7645-5498-0)

Quicken "X" For Dummies (0-7645-1666-3)

Stock Investing For Dummies (0-7645-5411-5)

Taxes For Dummies 2003 (0-7645-5475-1)

BUSINESS & CAREERS

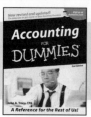

0-7645-5314-3   0-7645-5307-0   0-7645-5471-9

Also available:

Business Plans Kit For Dummies (0-7645-5365-8)

Consulting For Dummies (0-7645-5034-9)

Cool Careers For Dummies (0-7645-5345-3)

Human Resources Kit For Dummies (0-7645-5131-0)

Managing For Dummies (1-5688-4858-7)

QuickBooks All-in-One Desk Reference For Dummies (0-7645-1963-8)

Selling For Dummies (0-7645-5363-1)

Small Business Kit For Dummies (0-7645-5093-4)

Starting an eBay Business For Dummies (0-7645-1547-0)

HEALTH, SPORTS & FITNESS

0-7645-5167-1   0-7645-5146-9   0-7645-5154-X

Also available:

Controlling Cholesterol For Dummies (0-7645-5440-9)

Dieting For Dummies (0-7645-5126-4)

High Blood Pressure For Dummies (0-7645-5424-7)

Martial Arts For Dummies (0-7645-5358-5)

Menopause For Dummies (0-7645-5458-1)

Nutrition For Dummies (0-7645-5180-9)

Power Yoga For Dummies (0-7645-5342-9)

Thyroid For Dummies (0-7645-5385-2)

Weight Training For Dummies (0-7645-5168-X)

Yoga For Dummies (0-7645-5117-5)

Available wherever books are sold.
Go to www.dummies.com or call 1-877-762-2974 to order direct.

FOR DUMMIES®

A world of resources to help you grow

HOME, GARDEN & HOBBIES

Feng Shui For Dummies
0-7645-5295-3

Gardening For Dummies
0-7645-5130-2

Guitar For Dummies
0-7645-5106-X

Also available:

Auto Repair For Dummies
(0-7645-5089-6)

Chess For Dummies
(0-7645-5003-9)

Home Maintenance For Dummies
(0-7645-5215-5)

Organizing For Dummies
(0-7645-5300-3)

Piano For Dummies
(0-7645-5105-1)

Poker For Dummies
(0-7645-5232-5)

Quilting For Dummies
(0-7645-5118-3)

Rock Guitar For Dummies
(0-7645-5356-9)

Roses For Dummies
(0-7645-5202-3)

Sewing For Dummies
(0-7645-5137-X)

FOOD & WINE

Cooking For Dummies
0-7645-5250-3

Cookies For Dummies
0-7645-5390-9

Wine For Dummies
0-7645-5114-0

Also available:

Bartending For Dummies
(0-7645-5051-9)

Chinese Cooking For Dummies
(0-7645-5247-3)

Christmas Cooking For Dummies
(0-7645-5407-7)

Diabetes Cookbook For Dummies
(0-7645-5230-9)

Grilling For Dummies
(0-7645-5076-4)

Low-Fat Cooking For Dummies
(0-7645-5035-7)

Slow Cookers For Dummies
(0-7645-5240-6)

TRAVEL

Italy For Dummies
0-7645-5453-0

Hawaii For Dummies
0-7645-5438-7

Las Vegas For Dummies
0-7645-5448-4

Also available:

America's National Parks For Dummies
(0-7645-6204-5)

Caribbean For Dummies
(0-7645-5445-X)

Cruise Vacations For Dummies 2003
(0-7645-5459-X)

Europe For Dummies
(0-7645-5456-5)

Ireland For Dummies
(0-7645-6199-5)

France For Dummies
(0-7645-6292-4)

London For Dummies
(0-7645-5416-6)

Mexico's Beach Resorts For Dummies
(0-7645-6262-2)

Paris For Dummies
(0-7645-5494-8)

RV Vacations For Dummies
(0-7645-5443-3)

Walt Disney World & Orlando For Dummies
(0-7645-5444-1)

Available wherever books are sold. Go to www.dummies.com or call 1-877-762-2974 to order direct.

FOR DUMMIES®

Plain-English solutions for everyday challenges

COMPUTER BASICS

PCs FOR DUMMIES
A Reference for the Rest of Us!
Dan Gookin

0-7645-0838-5

The Flat-Screen iMac FOR DUMMIES
A Reference for the Rest of Us!
David Pogue

0-7645-1663-9

Windows XP ALL-IN-ONE DESK REFERENCE FOR DUMMIES
9 BOOKS IN 1
Woody Leonhard

0-7645-1548-9

Also available:

PCs All-in-One Desk Reference For Dummies (0-7645-0791-5)

Pocket PC For Dummies (0-7645-1640-X)

Treo and Visor For Dummies (0-7645-1673-6)

Troubleshooting Your PC For Dummies (0-7645-1669-8)

Upgrading & Fixing PCs For Dummies (0-7645-1665-5)

Windows XP For Dummies (0-7645-0893-8)

Windows XP For Dummies Quick Reference (0-7645-0897-0)

BUSINESS SOFTWARE

Excel 2002 FOR DUMMIES
A Reference for the Rest of Us!
Greg Harvey

0-7645-0822-9

Word 2002 FOR DUMMIES
A Reference for the Rest of Us!
Dan Gookin

0-7645-0839-3

Office XP 9 IN 1 DESK REFERENCE FOR DUMMIES
9 BOOKS IN 1

0-7645-0819-9

Also available:

Excel Data Analysis For Dummies (0-7645-1661-2)

Excel 2002 All-in-One Desk Reference For Dummies (0-7645-1794-5)

Excel 2002 For Dummies Quick Reference (0-7645-0829-6)

GoldMine "X" For Dummies (0-7645-0845-8)

Microsoft CRM For Dummies (0-7645-1698-1)

Microsoft Project 2002 For Dummies (0-7645-1628-0)

Office XP For Dummies (0-7645-0830-X)

Outlook 2002 For Dummies (0-7645-0828-8)

Get smart! Visit www.dummies.com

- **Find listings of even more *For Dummies* titles**

- **Browse online articles**

- **Sign up for Dummies eTips™**

- **Check out *For Dummies* fitness videos and other products**

- **Order from our online bookstore**

Available wherever books are sold. Go to www.dummies.com or call 1-877-762-2974 to order direct.

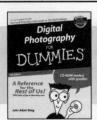

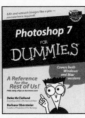

FOR DUMMIES®

The advice and explanations you need to succeed

SELF-HELP, SPIRITUALITY & RELIGION

0-7645-5302-X

0-7645-5418-2

0-7645-5264-3

Also available:

The Bible For Dummies
(0-7645-5296-1)

Buddhism For Dummies
(0-7645-5359-3)

Christian Prayer For
Dummies
(0-7645-5500-6)

Dating For Dummies
(0-7645-5072-1)

Judaism For Dummies
(0-7645-5299-6)

Potty Training For
Dummies
(0-7645-5417-4)

Pregnancy For Dummies
(0-7645-5074-8)

Rekindling Romance For
Dummies
(0-7645-5303-8)

Spirituality For Dummies
(0-7645-5298-8)

Weddings For Dummies
(0-7645-5055-1)

PETS

0-7645-5255-4

0-7645-5286-4

0-7645-5275-9

Also available:

Labrador Retrievers For
Dummies
(0-7645-5281-3)

Aquariums For Dummies
(0-7645-5156-6)

Birds For Dummies
(0-7645-5139-6)

Dogs For Dummies
(0-7645-5274-0)

Ferrets For Dummies
(0-7645-5259-7)

German Shepherds For
Dummies
(0-7645-5280-5)

Golden Retrievers For
Dummies
(0-7645-5267-8)

Horses For Dummies
(0-7645-5138-8)

Jack Russell Terriers For
Dummies
(0-7645-5268-6)

Puppies Raising &
Training Diary For
Dummies
(0-7645-0876-8)

EDUCATION & TEST PREPARATION

0-7645-5194-9

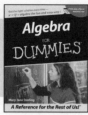

0-7645-5325-9

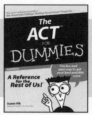

0-7645-5210-4

Also available:

Chemistry For Dummies
(0-7645-5430-1)

English Grammar For
Dummies
(0-7645-5322-4)

French For Dummies
(0-7645-5193-0)

The GMAT For Dummies
(0-7645-5251-1)

Inglés Para Dummies
(0-7645-5427-1)

Italian For Dummies
(0-7645-5196-5)

Research Papers For
Dummies
(0-7645-5426-3)

The SAT I For Dummies
(0-7645-5472-7)

U.S. History For Dummies
(0-7645-5249-X)

World History For
Dummies
(0-7645-5242-2)